"James Kenyon's vivid description tonic for those craving a connectic chores are told in such detail that working alongside young Jimmy as he milks the cows by hand, cleans the chicken house, or weeds the garden with his puppy by his side. We're invited to experience the death of a favorite horse as well as the excitement of this author's first kiss. Reality will bring laughs and tender moments as you work your way through this portrayal of a life well lived."

> Marci Penner, Executive Director,
> Kansas Sampler Foundation, and author of
> the *Kansas Guidebook for Explorers* and
> *8 Wonders of Kansas Guidebook*

"I have known Jim, or Jimmy as we called him, for many years, and it is a pleasure for me to endorse this book.

"This book is absolutely a 'must read.' If the reader was born and raised on a farm in northwest Kansas during the 1950s, this book will bring back many memories—some humorous and others so poignant they might still bring a tear or two. Even if not raised on a farm, a reader will gain much information about crops, farm animals, and the people who raise them. Farm families are one of a kind. Whether the reader was raised on a farm or in a city, he will appreciate this book.

> Mary Lou Pennington,
> Retired English Teacher, Bogue, Kansas

"James Kenyon's stories explore that promising decade between first memory and adolescence. Kenyon lived his preteen years on a farm in rural Kansas during a special time when preschool meant hours riding on his father's knee while they plowed a field together, and life lessons began with raising a calf, herding and milking the cattle, and selling eggs door-to-door. This was a simpler time when a boy grew up with his dog and his wagon and played baseball with his pals and sometimes (not often) parted with a nickel for a bottle of ice-cold orange pop. Readers will enjoy spending a quiet afternoon with Kenyon and will carry with them a sense of peace and well-being long after the final story is told."

> Mike Graves, author of *To Leave a
> Shadow*, a 2015 Kansas Notable Book

"If you are or were a city kid who wouldn't know an udder from a fresh-laid egg . . . If you didn't play something called midget basketball . . . If you never joined something called 4-H . . . Well—

you *have* to read James Kenyon's slender collection of first person stories, *A Cow for College*. You have lots to learn, some chuckles to enjoy and share, and you will get some appreciation that, 'Wow, farm kids had to sweat and get their hands dirty!'

"City kids, young and old, just might understand rural life better and develop more appreciation for what's being lost in America now that one-family farms of a few hundred acres are disappearing and corporate-style agriculture is winning. Especially in western Kansas, villages like Bogue are vanishing, and inter-connected, genuine community with them. Kenyon's home town of 300 in 1950 has 150 people left today. Most have thinning grey hair. Many small schools have closed. The few kids in or near town are bused to bigger schools, often miles away.

"Even if you were a farm kid who lived near a village of 300 and had just three girls in your entire class to flirt with (as 'Jimmy' did) – well, you owe yourself a memory rejuvenator. You'll remember when you tried to get independent-minded cows to go where you wanted and got kicked for your effort. You will remember your tears when a favorite pet or animal breathed its last breath before you were ready. (Oh, and if you live near Bogue, then or now, you'll recognize some names. Read the book!)"

> Bob Hooper, former English teacher,
> Bogue High; former public librarian;
> columnist, *The Hays Daily News*

"James Kenyon has put together a *wonderful* collection of stories detailing American rural life during a much simpler time in our history. The tales are also timeless and allow us to relive special moments and milestones in life—the pangs of first love; having a pet so special it becomes part of the family; the first moment when a youth understands death is part of the cycle of life; learning that faith, family, and belief in oneself can guide us through even the roughest of times; and other life-lessons as well. Bravo to James Kenyon for these exquisite slices of life!"

> Jeffrey S. Copeland, author of *Inman's War: A Soldier's Story of Life in a Colored Battalion in WWII*; *Shell Games: The Life and Times of Pearl McGill, Industrial Spy and Pioneer Labor Activist*; *Ain't No Harm to Kill the Devil: The Life and Times of John Fairfield, Abolitionist for Hire*

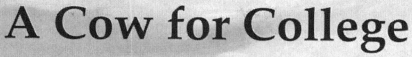

A Cow for College
and Other Stories of 1950s Farm Life

James Kenyon

To Skylar O'Brien — my beautiful California gal.
Your experiences as a "city girl" are so important to the life and future you will have. Treasure each day and enjoy your special family, dog, and friends.

Farm boys and girls had such an exposure to animals and cesnally many causeus in school and ball teams. Egg fights, bike races, "red rover", "annie-over", crack the whip, crazy eight, dominos, checkers, lemon ade — ice cream socials, and pat luck's in the park, hide and go seek — Wow what a life
Love and Happy trails
Uncle James Kenyon

Meadowlark (an imprint of Chasing Tigers Press)
Meadowlark-books.com
PO Box 333
Emporia, Kansas

Cover art by Barbara Steward Kenyon

Interior art by John Kenyon

ISBN: 978-0-9966801-4-1

Library of Congress Control Number: 2017952102

A Cow for College

and Other Stories of 1950s Farm Life

James Kenyon

A MEADOWLARK BOOK

Contents

Welcome Reader,

Thank you for joining me on this journey of remembrance of growing up in 1950s rural America. This is an account of my childhood, a young farm boy raised on the high plains of western Kansas, a remarkable setting where African Americans, Kentuckians, English Rhode Islanders, and French Acadians shared a small corner of the world. This space was all we knew and it meant everything to us. It is written about a rare time in America when there was no war. It was an age of innocence on the farm.

My parents were high school sweethearts from the age of sixteen. My mother's father, John Gibbins, was the first principal of Bogue Rural High School, the school I attended, and from which I eventually graduated. My parents married ten years after high school and had four children. As a couple, they farmed and survived the Great Depression, the Dirty Thirties, and World War II, which gradually brought an improvement in commodity prices for cattle, hogs, and wheat and made our lives easier.

I was born at the end of the 1940s when my mother was forty-two years old. Being the baby of a family of four had some advantages. My parents were older, more experienced, and maybe not as tough on the tag-a-long child. My brother, Claude Ritchey, was thirteen years old when I was born and nearly perfect in every endeavor. At least, that is what this adoring little brother thought. Claude graduated from medical school during the 1950s, the years in which this story takes place.

I can still see the bouncing, serpentine movements of the solitary jackrabbit running away over the short buffalo grass. Its tall ears were the last thing to disappear over a rocky knoll. I can still see the tadpoles blowing bubbles and churning the shallow water of the grader ditch. I can still hear the meadowlark sing—its yellow chest and black, v-shaped markings prominent—as it pauses on the ever-present wild sunflowers. The shallow stream meanders by the sandbars on its way across the flat meadow. Minnows dart upstream for the invisible plankton they engulf. The grasshoppers flip and jump as I, the intruder, walk through the knee-high bluestem grass. The talking killdeer scurries along the shoreline of the centuries-old buffalo wallow that collects the runoff from a recent gulley washer. The sunsets, an orange delight, are joined by the contrails of a massive air force training jet, painting the sky with dazzling white streaks. These visions are imprinted on my mind and heart for the rest of my life.

This story is composed of memories, all true stories from my life of growing up in rural America. I share many childhood lessons learned along the way. I hope you, the reader, enjoy the look back with me, and perhaps learn a little something to carry on with you, as well.

Sincerely,
James Kenyon

THE EARLY SETTLERS OF GRAHAM COUNTY, KANSAS

"Give me your tired, your poor, your huddled masses yearning to be free."

from The New Colossus, by Emma Lazarus

They all came—former slaves, Acadians, and an old horse trainer from Rhode Island. They were but a few of the nearly 200,000 homesteaders to stake a claim on the High Plains of Kansas in the 1870s and 1880s.

These homesteaders came to a land that had experienced monumental events in the preceding two decades. The Santa Fe Trail, the Kansas-Nebraska Act of 1854, Boarder Ruffians, Jayhawkers, John Brown's raid on Harpers Ferry in 1859, Beecher's Bibles, Kansas statehood in 1861, Quantrill's Raid on Lawrence, the Civil War, the Chisolm Trail, and the railroads all made this a land of blood, sweat, and tears. All the homesteaders had to do was pay a ten-dollar filing fee, build a house, and live on 160 acres for five years to make the land of promise become their own.

They came for the land—Volga Germans, Russian Mennonites, Dutch, English, Swedes, Norwegians, Danish, Bohemian-Czechs, French Swiss, German Swiss, German Hungarians, Bukovina Germans, Austrians, poor New Englanders, New York Irish, Pennsylvania Dutch, River Brethren from the Susquehanna River, and impoverished farmers from Minnesota—all were lured to Kansas by the prospect of free land in the Homestead Act of 1862.

Located in the northwest corner of Kansas, Graham County is four counties in from Colorado and two counties down from Nebraska. The first recorded female came to the county in 1870. By the 1880 census, there were 3,200 inhabitants in this thirty-square-mile county.

In the last year of the eighteenth century, a baby named Barber Kenyon was born to a Rhode Island farmer. George Washington died that same year, in 1799. That was also the year that the dynamic patriot leader, Patrick Henry, of "Give me liberty or give me death" fame died.

Barber Kenyon struggled to provide a living for his family. His first wife died, leaving him with three children to raise. His second wife was younger than his oldest son. He left Rhode Island to homestead for free land in Kansas at the age of 75 with his young wife and three children. Barber Kenyon's family chose to settle in Nicodemus Township.

On the eastern border of Graham County, the emancipated slave town of Nicodemus was named after the legendary figure, Nicodemus, who came to America on a slave ship and later purchased his freedom. African Americans migrated from Kentucky and settled in Kansas in 1877, having been encouraged by fliers and handbills touting the free land out West. Many had been the slaves of none other than the seventeenth president of the United States, Andrew Johnson. Some of the emancipated slaves had his surname because that was the method of naming children on the plantations in slave states.

"I am anxious to reach your state . . . because of the sacredness of her soil by the blood of humanitarians for the cause of freedom," wrote S.L. Johnson, a black Louisianan, in a letter to Kansas Governor St. John in 1879.

The Western Eden, self-governed, opportunity-filled—these were all exaggerated qualities spread on the railroads by flyers, hand-bills, and circulars across the eastern and southern states. One flyer was headlined:

ALL COLORED PEOPLE
GO TO KANSAS
On September 5, 1877
CAN DO FOR $5.00

The adjacent homesteads to Nicodemus attracted French Acadian farmers from Canada. Their Catholic religion unified this new community; the St. Joseph Catholic Church rivalled any church in the country with its beauty, elegance, and architectural magnificence.

The town of Damar was seven miles from Bogue. It was one-hundred percent French Acadian Catholic. There never was, and to this day never has been a Protestant living in Damar. The Frenchmen had come to this region to homestead in the 1880s. They came on faith and hope for a better life, just like the emancipated slaves came to Nicodemus. Following World War II, the men returned to this small, agrarian community to find limited opportunity. The farms were not large enough to support multiple families. With so many children, there was not enough land to follow the time-honored tradition of handing down land to the male children. Many of these young men took up trades in carpentry, finishing, painting, and plumbing.

For many years, Damar did not have a high school. All of those who desired further education went to school in Bogue. During the depression years, the town finally built their own high school. Athletic rivalries quickly became strong between the two little towns.

The wonderful French surnames of Desmarteau, Desaire, Belisle, LaBarge, Brault, Gosselin, Newell, Desbien, Conyac, Benoit, Davignon, and Simoneau can still be found in Graham County. These names have endured 200 to 300 years in North America. Most prejudice has disappeared in the last sixty years as intermarriage has diluted the mistrust and differences. The depopulation of the High Plains, at the same time, has caused all the people from that area to unite. Graham county has lost the largest percentage of population from 1990-2010 of any county in the United States. The average age of the surviving population would rival any advanced senior center in Florida.

They do not know where the future lies, but neither did those brave souls who first came and settled the area. The French, former slaves, and the poor Rhode Island family—they all came, settled, and shared the good times, the droughts, the depression, the grasshoppers, and the dust bowl. They all lived and raised families together in this small corner of the Kansas High Plains.

Barber Kenyon's son, Benedict, who had accompanied the family west from Rhode Island, lobbied for a high school and served on the first school board. The Bogue Rural High School provided for the area's secondary education. Benedict's grandson, the author of this book, attended that high school.

A young French student in 1935 said, "We are one-third black, one-third white, and one-third French!"

What a melting pot!

A COW FOR COLLEGE

Before we entered grade school, each of my siblings and I were given a heifer calf when it was born. We each had our choice of which calf we wanted. We would watch it nurse and grow through the summer while grazing on the buffalo grass pastures. There was only one day each year that we were allowed to skip school. That was the day of the fall roundup.

For roundup, all the cows and their calves were surrounded and guided into the catch pen alley and into the stockyards. Those riding the horses had the best seat in the roundup. Those on foot would help by blocking and waving their arms. A successful roundup required getting all the cows and calves in the catch-pen on the first try. The sounds of cowboys yelling "yep, yep, yep cow" and "sa-boss sa-boss" or "high-o, high-o cattle" could be heard above the bawling and bellowing of the little doggies in the early morning air.

The cows were cut back one at a time through the swinging gate. The big, slow moving bulls with their curled horns were kept back to separate them from the cows and calves. The children helped separate the calves from their mothers. We helped load the bawling calves onto the truck to be transported to the home place and unloaded into the closed weaning pen. Many of the mother cows would line up on the outside of the fence, looking for their calves. Their bellowing was painful to hear as they were having to give up their calves for good. As a young farm boy tasked at helping for this important job, I had to be careful because all the dust in the air made a charging cow difficult to see. One had to be agile and alert at all times to avoid a kick from a cow or calf.

My dad fed his cows better than his brothers and the neighbors fed theirs. The corn and stalks were chopped and made into silage. This green chop was placed in an upright stave silo or a pit where it would undergo anaerobic fermentation. The smell of silage is not unlike the mixture of sweet and sour pork. It was a tannish brown and cows loved the sweet acidic taste. Silage and alfalfa hay were fed in combination and were ideal for a nutritionally balanced ration.

On mornings when Dad loaded the pickup truck with silage, he put ten to fifteen bales of hay on top. He honked the horn and I would come running to ride north with him to feed the cattle. Dad and I talked about the cows and where we would move them next when the grass got short. We often speculated about any new babies that might have been born overnight. We discussed the weather and if we needed to leave more or less food because of the cold weather forecast.

At the cow pasture, I got out eagerly to open the four-strand barbed wire gate. Dad rotated where we fed the cattle. He selected places where the brome grass was still tall. Some of the grasses were not the cows' favorites to eat and were left to get tall. When putting the hay and feed on this taller grass, it encouraged the cows to forage on this grass, too.

With the pickup in its lowest gear, I steered the truck to keep it going straight while Dad got in the back to throw out the silage. This was my job from the time I was four years old. I was to not touch the gas pedal until I was older and could judge the acceleration. To attract the cows to come for their feed, we honked the horn on the blue pickup in a rhythm known to our cows. They saw the truck and came running. The calves frolicked and kicked up their heels with excitement. I had an eye for identifying which calf belonged to which momma cow. Their markings and patterns were all unique, even though Herefords were basically red and white.

Cutting the twine around the hay bales with his knife, Dad alternated feeding on each side of the pickup truck. First, he would throw several wedges to the left followed by three or four pitchforks of silage on the top. This kept the silage from being thrown directly on the open dirt. The first greedy cows rushed eagerly for the feed. The next hay and silage would go to the right side of the truck and Dad kept alternating sides until the pickup was empty.

After feeding, we circled around to get a count on the cows. The exact number would have to be present and accounted for or we had to go looking for them. During calving season, there would be a calf or two born each day. A cow who was off by herself in the tall grass would have a calf by the next day. When we counted the cows, we checked those that looked like they were making bag and "springing" under the tail area. The swollen labia and a clear stringy mucous discharge indicated their cervix was expanding as the cow was close to calving.

I always thought the most beautiful calf was a Hereford with its dark red body and white face, neck, belly, and tip of the tail. A first-time heifer calving was a wonder in animal instincts. She could not seem to believe that this wet, moving, gawky calf had just emerged from her birth canal. She would look around behind her and nervously moo, almost acting afraid. Carefully, she would smell the newborn with the placenta still attached. She licked it, and the bond was set. Each baby had its own smell, and a cow could identify her calf by smell alone.

My oldest sister Janie's calf grew and became a wonderful, docile cow. Each year her cow's calf was sold separately and the proceeds would go into her college savings account. The approximately three-hundred dollars earned each year almost paid for a year of college in 1950. I got to help take care of Janie's cow and was so amazed by her productivity. She had classic Hereford markings. She had a small nub of a horn that had regrown from a botched dehorning as a calf. Her deep red hair was accented by a nearly pearly iridescent white face and withers strip along her cervical spine. Janie had not named the cow, but I called her Old Girl. Janie was a teenager by the time I got to help take care of the cows.

Cows do not live much past ten years of age on the arid high plains. The grass they eat is so short that they must forage close to the ground and the sand helps erode their teeth. The term "gummer" means that they had started losing their teeth. Gummers were not able to bite off the grass as well and lost weight and were not able to breed back and give milk for a calf.

Old Girl defied the odds. I'm sure she had lost most of her teeth, but she maintained her body weight well. Except for a slightly dished face, sunken eyes, and a limp on her back leg, there were no other visible signs of her age.

My brother Claude was lucky. He had been given two calves. This may have been serendipitous, because he went on to medical school for a total of eight years of college. The income from two calves helped with this college plan. His two calves grew into an unusual pair. Goldie, as I called her, was a stunning yellowish-red Hereford. She had a small brockle around one eye. If she were a person, she would have been called a good-looking woman. She walked with confidence. She pushed the more timid cows away from the silage piles. Her calves were spitting images of her markings, and they were the first born each spring. They were the biggest and fastest growing calves, and they showed off their athleticism. The fast growth of offspring was also indicative that Goldie was a good milker. Her faucets were perfectly shaped and this made them easy for the calves to nurse.

Claude's second cow was dark red with a typical Hereford white face, neck, belly, and legs. The red on the neck came forward more than others in the herd, so I called her Red Neck. Red Neck's body was compact and stout. She was always in good flesh and even fat compared to the rest of the herd. When she walked into the feeding line, the other cows took notice. They quickly grabbed a bite for the road, trying to avoid a head butt in the ribs from Red Neck. Claude's second heifer was notorious for her head butts to get all of the feed in the pile on the ground. The other cows did not like her and gave her plenty of ground.

Goldie and Red Neck each had a vice. They were "breechey" as my dad said. Sometimes he called them fence jumpers or old rips. They started getting out when our pastures were getting short of grass in the heat of the summer. Like a magnet, they could find a loose barbed wire or downed fence. They would go to the greener pasture, getting into my Uncle Lyle's or the neighboring Worcester's herd in the adjacent pastures along Spring Creek.

Country cows will spread out over a half-section when grazing. Dad and I drove all over the pasture counting the cows. When our count was off by one or two, we immediately drove the fence line to find the broken post or downed wire. We would have to go home and load up our horse, Tony, to find the old rips. The neighbors would help us shepherd them back to our corral.

My dad did not tolerate cows who got out. The penalty for such actions warranted a yoke around the neck. There was a standard metal yoke that could be fitted to the size of the cow's neck and bolted in place. It had two metal projections off the dorsal and ventral portions of the neck band. These projections stuck up and down by a foot and had a hook at the end pointing forward. When the cow put her head between two barbed wires, these hooks were supposed to catch on the wires and deter any forward pushing on the wires by the cow. These two old pros just turned their heads sideways and pushed forward, breaking the wire.

Dad had another method in his bag of tricks. He preferred the homemade yoke. He wrapped four strands of barbed wire around the cow's neck tightly and secured it with baling wire. The two ends extended three feet dorsally and ventrally to mimic the metal yoke projections. When the cow was released from the catch-chute, she had to drag this bottom barbed wire. Though it looked hideous, this yoke was the fix for the fence marauders.

When it was my turn, I chose a calf from a beautiful Hereford cow. The momma had a distinct white marking that ran down the whole length of her back to her tail. We called these cattle linebackers because of this white line of hair. The purest Hereford, show-cattle breeders thought this was a defect to the breed and selected away from this trait. My observation was that most linebacker cows were stout, good milkers, and produced exceptionally big and strong calves. For this reason, I picked the linebacker's plump calf which had perfect body confirmation. She, too, was a linebacker. I named her Happy and placed in the keeper heifer pen with all the other replacement heifers. She was easy to spot because of her white lined back. She was very calm and had a pretty face. She always seemed be smiling.

We routinely mated the first calf heifers with a Black Angus bull. This resulted in smaller calves and made the delivery easier for the little heifers. This cross seemed to work for Happy. She had a pretty black and white faced calf the next spring. Her milk production seemed adequate and her teats seemed to be wet from the calf nursing. Yet, something was wrong. Her calves did not grow well. By the end of the summer grazing, a dark, dirty, scruffy mark started appearing on Happy's white brisket area. When she was placed in a restraining chute, it was easy to see that this dirty neck was because she had lice. Lice were an opportunistic, bloodsucking parasite. The lice attacked the weaker animals that may have had compromised immune systems. Dad and I doused Happy with louse powder monthly. We just could not seem to completely get her free of those bloodsucking, biting, varmints. Cattle rubbers filled with diesel fuel and fly and lice insecticides worked for the other cows, but not for Happy.

One morning when feeding the cattle, our numbers were off by one cow. I knew from the day before that Old Girl was springing very heavy. I looked for her intently as we took our second count.

Dad said, "How many did you get?"

I finished counting the cows and said, "That's 69, 70, and 71 . . . Yup, we are one short. I think it is Old Girl."

"You know, Son, I believe you are right. That is not like her. She is always so proud to bring her newborn up to the feed line," Dad said with a worried look on his face. We both hopped into the truck to go look for Janie's Old Girl. Dad mumbled as we searched all of the draws and canyons.

"There she is, Daddy," I said and excitedly pointed to a spot high up on a bluff among the prairie dog mounds. She was lying on her sternum when we reached her. Behind her lay a huge, dead calf. She had turned around and licked it dry, but it appeared to have been born dead.

"This is not good, Son," Dad said, shaking his head.

"What do you mean? We can always buy another calf and put it on her," I said as I reached down to pet Old Girl's forehead.

"I'm afraid she has calving paralysis or she has broken her hip," he said as he examined her back end and legs. Old Girl could not get up. Her back legs did not have any feeling. She tried to get up on her front legs, but nothing was working in the rear.

We went to the creek to fill a bucket with spring water. Old Girl drank it eagerly and we had to fill it one more time to satisfy her thirst. She had struggled all night and was weak. We gave her some leftover hay and silage, but she did not seem interested. We loaded the dead calf to take it away so that the coyotes would not get it.

I talked to Old Girl and told her, "We'll be back tomorrow to bring you some more water and feed. I'm so sorry about your calf. He was beautiful and the biggest one you have ever had."

Each morning for the next two weeks, Dad and I took a special silage and hay mixture and water to the poor downer, Old Girl. At first, it seemed hopeful that there was some progress. There were signs that she had moved during the night, but she became weaker by the day. One morning, it was obvious that she was not going to live much longer.

I tried to console her saying, "Old Girl, I'm so sorry. You have been such a wonderful cow. Dad says you have had seventeen calves and never lost one until this. I will tell Janie that you are still such a gorgeous girl." Petting her face in parting, I knew she would be dead by the next morning.

The next morning, frost sparkled in the sunlight as we approached Old Girl on the ridge. She was flat out and had died during the night.

"Daddy," I asked. "What is it like to die? I really loved her."

"You know, I can't say for sure. I think Old Girl was so tired from her struggles to get up and her age that she was not in much pain," Dad said. My father never showed much emotion, but his quietness told me that he was sad, too.

Years later, as a veterinarian, I understood that cows that had names always had a story behind them. They had special personalities, antics, and traits. Sixty years later, I can still see Old Girl laying up on that bluff with her paralyzed legs; Happy, with her darkened lice infested brisket; and those two old rips, Goldie and Red Neck, dragging around their homemade yokes.

A cow is just another of God's beautiful creatures that man is so fortunate to know.

სოღ

2 –3 –1

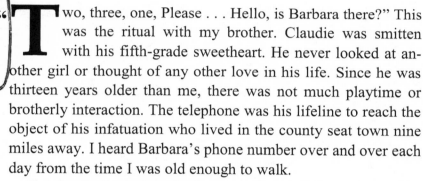

"Two, three, one, Please . . . Hello, is Barbara there?" This was the ritual with my brother. Claudie was smitten with his fifth-grade sweetheart. He never looked at another girl or thought of any other love in his life. Since he was thirteen years older than me, there was not much playtime or brotherly interaction. The telephone was his lifeline to reach the object of his infatuation who lived in the county seat town nine miles away. I heard Barbara's phone number over and over each day from the time I was old enough to walk.

Our family had a crank phone on the wall in a stained oak box. We were on a party line. The caller would pick up the receiver which was on the end of a cord attached to a Y-shaped hook on the side of the telephone box. The caller held the receiver to his ear to listen if one of the other seven neighbors was using the line before cranking the small metal handle on the right side of the phone box to get the operator. The bell at the top rang and an operator answered and said, "Number, Please." It was not important to know from where and who this operator was, but she somehow took our line and plugged it into a circuit bank opening to the sprocket of the number we were calling. When this connection and electrical current were completed, that person's phone rang in their home. Since we were in such a rural area, the party line (multiple homes on the same circuit) was normal operating procedure. We could call others on our circuit by knowing their phone number and rotating the lever to the proper long and short bell sound. Our number was two long rings and two short rings, 2 –2 –0 –4, commonly called two longs and two shorts. When the bell vibrated two long rings followed by two short rings, we knew to pick up the receiver to answer, speaking into the horizontal circular mouth piece that looked like a duck's beak. Others on our party line may have been a long and two short rings. Or two shorts and a long. Or even four short rings. When making a call out or when receiving a call, any of the other seven on the party line could pick up the receiver and listen to your conversation. Holding one hand over the horizontal mouthpiece mostly muffled any noise that was caused by listening in on someone else's conversation. We called those who listened in busy bodies. It was often said, "I can't tell you this because someone may be listening in." This comment alone might cause a clicking noise as the snoopy neighbor hung up their phone receiver. "They may still be listening in, so I can't tell you this yet, so I'll have to talk with you in person," was another reply that was heard often.

My brother's calls to Barbie were never a concern to him. He could have cared less if anyone was listening in on their love talks. "Do you love me?" "I love you. I love you! I love you! Smack. Smack!" More kissing and smooching noises, then a pause and nothing for thirty seconds. Then more smooching and a deep breathing as if resuscitation was taking place. "I'm not going to say anything until you do." This was followed by several minutes of breathing into the phone receiver, saying nothing. This really had to frustrate a busy body listening in on the conversation or anyone who needed to make a call out while those lovebirds tied up the line.

Sending Claude out to drive the tractor in the field was a futile effort. After he made a few rounds in the field with a plow or cultivator, he had to stop, come to the house and call 2 –3 –1.

My brother's love, Barbara, was a precious princess. She would never reach five-foot-tall, and she weighed about ninety pounds. She was smart as a whip, and her loving smile and beautiful face made me wish that I was old enough to have her for my girlfriend, too.

Barb and Claude. Claudie and Barbie. Their names seemed synonymous. You didn't hear one without the other. They went to college together at the University of Kansas. After their freshman year, they were married, both still eighteen years old. They seemed so grown up to me as a six-year-old ring bearer, holding up my end of the ceremony with a white satin ring pad for the wedding photos.

My dad was responsible for providing a car and some affordable means of housing for the newlyweds. He bought them a mobile home, which to me was a playhouse on wheels. Each fall he hitched up the pickup truck to the eight-foot-by-thirty-eight-foot blue mobile home and towed it the 270 miles of two-lane roads to Lawrence in eastern Kansas. In the spring, when the semester was done, Dad went back to the university in the pickup, jacked and hooked up the trailer, and pulled it back to the farm for the summer. A four-foot-deep hole would be dug for a waste cesspool, and the newlyweds were nuzzled in for the summer.

Claude was never destined to be a farmer. He had asthma and hay fever. If he wasn't coughing and sneezing, he was blowing mucous. (We were never allowed to say the gross word, "snot.") The wheat dust at harvest time set off two weeks of coughing, snorting, and misery for him. The alfalfa hay bales accentuated his problem. The hay dust wasn't much better for his asthma, so he was often relegated to less dusty jobs. His true love was in the little blue trailer, and he didn't need anything else.

The privacy of the newlyweds in the trailer was great, but they had to live with some of the more unusual noises that accompanied this setting. Our goofy dog, Jack, had an unusually long white tail. He crawled under the trailer at night because it was a cool, safe place to lie down. His thumping tail up under the bottom of the floor panels brought out a shout from my brother, "Jack, knock it off!" This resulted in silence for a few moments and then the act was repeated. Before long, Jack was tied up on a chain or shut in the cow barn for more peace and quiet at nights.

After living away from home, being brought back to the farm must have been a setback for the couple's privacy. I was a constant visitor to see Barbara, and she was a wonderful big sister-in-law. She talked to me like an adult and always had an activity to make the day fun. Whether it was drawing, painting, or games, I had her total attention and I was on cloud nine.

After two summers of moving the little house on wheels back and forth to college, it was pulled to Kansas City where Claude attended medical school. It made it back four years later, after medical school graduation, to sit in our backyard for a while longer. During those summers, my nephews—Jon, Chris, and Noel—and I used it as our getaway clubhouse. Sleeping in the trailer on the cool nights of the western Kansas plains was like sleeping under the open sky with a campfire crackling in the night. Dreaming about such a scene was fun, but sleeping inside with a carpet under us and the screens filtering out the mosquitos was even better. For the four young boys on an adventure, distant nighttime howling of coyotes made it seem safer inside. The hoot owl methodically called all night, singing a forlorn solo in a distant tree.

Without the lifeline of the party line and 2 −3 −1, this blue trailer may never have been a reality. The romance, the asthma, and medical school all paved the way for my brother to leave the farm behind for the wonderful suburban life of Kansas City with his childhood sweetheart.

ഇറയ

THE FARM DOG

During the twentieth century, all farms across the Midwest had a least one dog. Even during the Great Depression and Dust Bowl years of the 1930s, there was always a dog or two for the family to feed.

Rarely was a dog allowed in the house. It did not mean that the dog was not loved, it was simply the dog's place in the family structure. The bare, wooden, A-framed dog house out back with a chain to secure the dog to an iron stake was common. These dogs never saw a veterinarian in their lifetime. They ate table scraps and foraged for rabbits and small rodents. The grain elevator carried a fifty-pound bag of "el-cheapo" dog nuggets. Ralston Purina brand foods were only found in bigger cities. There were no vaccinations, no regular de-worming, no flea protection, and no dental care for the family pet.

There were the occasional purebred dogs, such as a German shepherd or collie, but most were just a great, all-American crossbreed. The litter of pups from the neighbor's female was shared with area farmers. The saying that "the mom came from a good home and the dad came from a good neighborhood" could not have been truer. This was not lack of care by the farmer and his family, a dog's place was simply outside. A dog followed his farmer closely as he worked around the barnyards and with the livestock. It waited patiently while the cows were being milked. The mutt regularly got a sample of the leftover milk, along with the table scraps from the evening supper.

Mashed potatoes, fat from the ham or steaks, and chicken bones and skin were normal offerings.

Names such as Shep, Red, Buster, and King were very common. The farm dog never got a bath, and yet could be in the mud one minute, dry off fast, and shed dirt from his hair and coat just by shaking and scratching.

Most dogs tolerated the myriad of farm cats who also vied for the table scraps, leftovers, and some daily helping of milk from the cows. The dogs often shared a bed or nest in the barn with a cat. It was not an uncommon scene to see a dog curled up in a comma position, lying on its side. The head and nose almost reached around to the back feet and numerous cats would be wrapped around him. The animals shared each other's warmth during the cold seasons and their common plight of the survival of the fittest.

Few dogs ever made it to old age or even into their teenage years. Farm accidents, death by car, or simply wandering off, never to come home again, were an expected part of a farm dog's life. No leaflets were posted on telephone poles looking for a lost dog. Chasing cars often ended in a premature end of life.

Dogs who liked chasing cars would hear a car coming down the road from a distance and lie coyly in the grader ditch, crouched down in the vegetation ready to spring out in pursuit of the speeding vehicle. This characteristic of a dog to chase cars has never been quite understood. One would think that the high mortality rate of being hit by the cars would have eliminated the gene that leads to chasing cars. There were some dogs that even bit at the rotating tire as if it were a demon they were attacking. Big dogs, fat dogs, little dogs—it didn't seem to matter. If they were a chaser, you could never stop them of the habit. There were times, if being hit or rolled wasn't fatal, that there seemed to be a parole time from the action. But within a few weeks of hobbling around or limping while they recovered from their bruises, the dog would soon be at it again, hiding in the ditch to attack the next rubber tire victim.

My first dog's name was Jack. We had a neighbor whose nephew, Dwight, lived in their small gardener house. I liked Dwight and thought his name was cool. By the time Jack came to us, Dwight had moved away, and I could not remember what his name was. I thought long and hard to come up with a name, and since I couldn't remember the name Dwight, Jack was the name I settled on for my puppy. Jack came to us from another neighbor's litter of pups. He was a Heinz 57 if ever there was a stereotype of a crossbred dog. Puppies, no matter what the breed or make, are irresistibly cute. To me, as a farm boy, the only other animal babies that could compare to puppies were kittens. Jack was a roly-poly pup. He was mostly white with a distinctive black patch eye. He could almost have been a clone of the RCA Victor logo dog or the white and black dog on the *Our Gang* movie set with Spanky, Alfalfa, and Buckwheat.

"Daddy, can he ride with us in the pickup to go to the cattle?" I begged. "He'll be so lonely if we leave him behind."

"Well, okay, but you will need to hold on to him so that he sits still and doesn't get nervous," Dad said as he gave into my wishes. This started many pickup rides with my pup accompanying us to town and riding to the pastures to feed the cattle and fix fence. Jack had a bad habit of passing gas on these pickup rides.

"Jack! Is that you again?" Dad barked. "You are the stinkiest dog I have ever known!" I snickered and Dad smirked as we both rolled down our windows. Old Jack seemed to bow his head in shame.

Jack liked to chase rabbits. He reminded me of the *Tawney Scrawny Lion* golden book where the tiger chased a different animal every day of the week, but never caught anything to eat. What a futile, pathetic exercise for Jack. All rabbits were safe because he never got within fifty feet of them. Jackrabbits, with their long legs and tall ears, were the cleverest. They seemed to bounce and weave just trying to entice their slower pursuer.

Jack was not the smartest dog on the block. He was what my dad called "worthless" with cattle. When he was around to help herd or chase the cattle, he had a one-way brain. That is, he al-

ways ran for the head and not the heels. Thus, the cow *always* veered in the wrong direction or tried to defend herself by butting or knocking Jack away with her head down and snorting sideways in defiance.

The great cattle dogs were those that nipped at the heels and slyly circled to get behind the cow. They were so evasive that a nip, or even the threat of the nip, would move a cow along with haste. These dogs could anticipate a cow kick and the cattle would not waste much time in even trying. Occasionally, even the best dog would take a cow's rear foot to the chops. It might yelp in pain and cower for a few seconds in agony. A bloody nose, mouth, or tongue didn't seem to deter a good cow dog, and it quickly recovered from the mishap. Shaking its head in determination, the dog was back at the task of helping the farmer move the cattle from one pen or location to another.

Milk cows were the easiest prey. Many, with their large milk bags or udders swinging like pendulums, didn't want to mess with dogs nipping at their rear ends. Milk cows were in daily contact with the dog, unlike the beef cattle who were in distant pastures. Moving milk cows down a lane to an adjoining paddock or wheat field was common. They were always moved after the morning milking to forage for the day. Then in the evening, going after the cows was my job. Being accompanied by a loyal dog made the task less mundane. By the time I was old enough to put a bridle on our horse, Tony, my walking days were a thing of the past.

Jack and I would sometimes go exploring. We went down to the river to play in the stream. Some dogs can avoid the sandburs on the ground or the ever-present Mexican burs that were along the railroad tracks. It seemed that old Jack was constantly stopping to pull out the burs from his feet with his teeth. After getting a bur, most dogs limped on three legs for a while until the sharp sticker dropped out on its own. Not Jack. Even the smallest sticker put him out of commission.

Every farmer who raised cattle had a similar operation. The cows grazed on pasture and their diets were supplemented with hay, silage, or forage during the winter months until the grass was available in early May. Dad was one of the few farmers who finished the weaned calves in the feedlot right on the farm-yard site. Feeding the yearlings from weaning weight up to 1,000 pounds took five to seven months. He often bought a load or two of feeder cattle to supplement our seventy calves to make a bigger feed lot.

Dogs had jobs on the farm, but they sometimes went out at night with other dogs and prowled. They acted like adolescent boys at times, behaving as if nothing good happened until dark. Chasing confined cattle or sheep in a pen or lot seemed to draw in the neighbors' dogs for this fun-but-dangerous act. One Sunday night after coming home from church service, my dad heard the steers nervously bellowing on the other side of the barn in the dry lot. They were running and circling frantically, and the dust was fogging the nighttime twilight. A few lights from town could be seen through the din and barking dogs in the act of cattle chasing were visible. Yelling in the dark didn't stop stampeding cattle. Dogs in the act did not hear, or at least they refused to stop in the heat of action. After seeing the chaos, Dad rushed to the house to get the gun.

"Jimmy. Why don't you stay here in the house," he directed me. "This is a very serious stampede, and I worry that this time those dang dogs are going to run the steers through the high fences. I don't know which way they may break through the fence, so it is just safer for you here," he warned.

Daddy slid a shell into the chamber and hurried out into the dusty darkness. Barking, bellowing, and the circling of the cattle and dogs was pandemonium. In the poor light, Dad couldn't make out the color of the dogs, just their flashing silhouettes. Bracing himself on a post, he raised the rifle and took a bead on one of the racing vandals. Suddenly, the barking stopped, and the dogs ran for safety.

All along, we had thought the brown stray dog that lived across the field was the ring-leader in these periodic cattle chasing episodes. Daddy walked out to the far side of the feedlot to find that it was my Jack who was dead. He carried my dog back to the house for me to see his limp body with the bloody patch on the side of his chest. Poor old Jack, with his white hair coat, became a victim that night. Daddy had not meant to shoot our dog. Jack was just in the wrong place at the wrong time.

My father said, "I am so sorry, Son. I couldn't make out the dogs in the night and I sure hate it that Jack was the one I hit." With tears rolling down the cheeks of my six-year-old face, I went out into the woods with my dad and dug a grave for my good old dog. After laying Jack to rest, the chasing events seemed to end.

This was a sad ending for Jack. To say that my dog was not too smart was an understatement. He probably had very few redeeming qualities, but his goofy black-patched eye and wagging tail endeared him to this farm boy's heart. I should add that he was nice to the cats.

Chasing cars and chasing cattle were two instincts, I learned early, that would lead to a farm dog's demise. This nature of dogs is still seen in our city dogs, as some will want to attack another dog or stranger walking near their turf. Many of these traits can be eliminated by selective breeding, but will never be bred out of dogs completely.

ဆာဘ

THE TRACTOR

"**J**immy, get your hat and let's get going. Daylight's burnin'!" That was my dad's way of calling me into the house to get me ready for a morning together on the big red tractor. "Do you have our water jug ready? And how about our lunch pails?" Even though I was not responsible for getting the water and lunch ready, this was standard procedure as we headed off to the field for a day on the tractor. Mother made our lunches and had them ready in the well-worn, metal pail. Apples, ham sandwiches, carrots, and cookies were a standard picnic lunch. The water jug was a large gallon jar wrapped in burlap to help keep the contents cold in the blistering heat of the day.

"Yup," I replied quickly. "I'm just pulling on my cowboy boots now. The water jug is ready and Mom has our lunch. Are we going to be gone all day?"

"Naw, probably not, but having something to eat never hurts when we get going," Dad would say.

He was always Dad to me, and occasionally Daddy, but never Papa or Pops. A quiet, strong man, my dad had seen the good and bad times of farming. My father was raised in a large family that had as many as thirty horses to help farm. His three brothers and one sister all lived within a half mile of our farm on the edge of town. Aunts, uncles, and cousins made a great extended family.

Dad started farming just after World War I and survived the Great Depression in the 1930s. World War II had brought better commodity prices. The climate in the 1950s was good for crops and the economy improved for both livestock and grain farmers.

By the time I was three years old, riding on the tractor was a joyful, daily occurrence. At first, I sat on my dad's overalls-clad lap. Both of us wore identical straw hats to shade our faces and necks from the ever-present sun.

Kansas was the sunflower state, but it could also be called simply the sun state. Its capital, Topeka, has more days of sunshine than any other state capital in the United States. So much for Florida's claim to being the sunshine state!

My dad wore his blue denim, Big Smith overalls every day. His apparel never altered. The snap breast pockets on the bib contained a stubby pencil and important note pads filled with paper and small clippings. His watch was suspended by a braided leather strand attached to the suspender and neatly tucked into the almost invisible watch pocket on the side of the bib. His long-sleeved, blue-cotton shirts covered his arms down to the wrists. The kid-leather, yellow gloves protected his hands from the grease, oil, and the many dings and scrapes a farmer gets from maneuvering his hands in precariously sharp and dangerous work situations. This true farmer never, ever donned blue Levi jeans or a short-sleeved work shirt. His straw hat had a small, greenish, polarized plastic insert in the front of the brim, which allowed some sunlight in, much like a sunroof on sport cars.

"So where are we heading today, Daddy?" I eagerly asked. Every day was different and we always had a plan.

"Well, Son, we have our work cut out for us. First, we have to take the pickup to the Griffey Place and unhook it from the tractor. With the big rains yesterday north of the cattle on Spring Creek, I worry that the fence across the Creek may have washed out. If it did, and the water goes down quickly, the cattle will be able to get out and will be over in Uncle Lyle's milo," he said, plotting out our morning schedule.

"Great! On that west fence line, over by the creek, there is that thicket of sand plums that should be ripe for picking," I said as I plotted out scenes in my mind.

The trek to the Griffey Place was slow with the pickup and the wheat drill being pulled behind the tractor. Every Western Meadowlark in the county must have been singing and fluttering from fence post to fence post as we passed. The sunflowers were losing their leaves and their golden petals had seen better days. The larks with their gorgeous yellow breasts topped by the distinctive black bibs seemed to know that fall was in the air. Meadowlarks never flew in a straight line as they weaved and bobbed in erratic patterns from fence post to shrub and then on to a sunflower stalk. The heat of the summer had passed, leaving them with plenty of seeds and grains in the fields to eat.

Our tractors and combines in the 1950s and 60s did not have cabs surrounding the platforms. They were open-air dust magnets, and insects swarmed when the wind was not blowing. Just like the abundance of sun, the wind was a constant on the high plains. We often said that in a week's time, the wind blew out of the west for three days, remained calm for one day about midweek, and turned around and blew out of the east for the next three days. When plowing or pulling a disc implement in the fields, this ever-present wind would blow the dust in our faces or backs, depending on which direction we were going.

Terracing became a method of soil conservation post WWII. High bank terraces, or dikes, meandered over the fields, mapped by the contour lines and topography. These terraces held rain water back during heavy rains, which otherwise would have gone gushing down the sides of the hills. On the High Plains conserving moisture was a must. Before terracing, erosion and ditches were formed and the top-soil ended up in the draws and the neighboring farmers' bottom-ground, much like an alluvial plain in the delta.

"Daddy, why did they make these terraces so close together?" I would ask.

"You know, Son, I have wondered that same thing. It sure seems that they could have mapped one less on this hillside. I believe that each terrace has to be two feet lower than the one above it, so when there is a steeper side hill, the terraces are closer together. I didn't have much say in the platting and design of the terraces. The agriculture office in Hill City makes those decisions, and we farmers just have to go along. They give us some incentive, but not much," he explained to me. There was never anything that my Dad told me that escaped my memory or understanding.

Driving a tractor around these contour dikes took care and attention to the front tire positioning. If there was water or mud on the uphill side and the tractor tire got too close, the tractor could get stuck clear up to the back axle. Not only did this leave deep ruts in the fields and terrace bottoms, it required walking back to a neighbor's farm to call for help. Another tractor was summoned and a heavy log chain attached to the hitch in attempt to dislodge the iron horse stuck in the mud. Precious time was lost and daylight was burnin'.

The sun and wind dried the sandy loam soil rapidly. After the occasional shower, it took only a few hours of sunlight to dry the soil so that a tractor could begin its work. I say occasional shower because the average rainfall in the arid, high plains was less than twenty inches per year. We always said this annual rainfall came in two cloudbursts, one in May and the other in September. Conserving the soil moisture was necessary if a crop was to be grown. Wheat thrived in this environment.

Hard Red Winter Wheat was brought to America by the Russian Mennonite immigrants in the 1870s. The seeds were sown in the ground in late September when the days were cooler, but the warm, moist soil helped the seed to germinate and sprout. In about a week, the small green shoots could be seen poking through the crust. Proper seed-bed preparation was needed to get a good stand. The wheat drill had from sixteen to thirty-two discs that penetrated the upper two inches of the soil. A coiled nozzle leading from the overhead seed box directed the falling kernel into this open furrow. Once the seed was dropped, a packer wheel closed the furrow and packs the moist soil around the seed. This remains the basic process even to this day.

Drilling wheat was just the beginning of the nine-month process of reaping what was sowed. "Daddy, how do you know how many seeds to plant?" I asked in wonderment.

"Well, it comes from experience," he explained. "The meter box cog in the planter is set so that only so many seeds can drop down the coil per revolution. Depending on the variety of seed and how much moisture is in the topsoil, I set the number of seeds to be planted per acre."

"Got it," was my quick response and understanding.

The rowing of dew-covered seedlings that glistened when I looked east into the rising sun was a mesmerizing sight and proof that new life had started. This was only equaled by the sight of a baby calf running to nurse his mother or the monarch butterfly lightly touching down on a lavender alfalfa bloom in a solid field of purple. Fall planting needed only a shower or two within a couple of months to get good roots and allow the plant to spread on the surface. It would "stool" or leaf out soon to cover the drill ridges. A solid field of dark green wheat by Thanksgiving was the answer to a farmer's prayer and hard work.

Wind erosion during the dry season could blow the seeds away. It was another problem if the seeds were buried too deep. In the event of rain, a hard crust could form that prevented the sprout from penetrating the surface. Pheasants and Bobwhite quail got their portion of the wheat by scratching down to feast on the succulent seeds. Drought caused the top soil to be very fine and powdery. Dust storms were whipped up by the ever-gentle breeze and the more powerful gales cut off the sprout at the surface and destroyed its growth. The parable in Matthew 13 was completely understood by a Kansas wheat farmer. Jesus said, "Listen! A farmer went out to plant some seeds. As he scattered them across his field, some seeds fell on the footpath, and the birds came and ate them. Other seeds fell on shallow soil with the underlying rock. The seeds sprouted quickly because the soil was shallow. But the plants soon wilted under the hot sun, and since they didn't have deep roots, they died. Other seeds fell among thorns that grew up and choked out the tender plants. Still other seeds fell on fertile soil, and they produced a crop that was thirty, sixty, and even a hundred times as much as had been planted. Anyone with ears to hear should listen and understand." (Holy Bible: New Revised Version, American Bible Society, NY, 1966/1971/1976)

No two years are the same. The farmer deals with the elements and never brags that the growing season is perfect, because it only invites disappointment with the turn of the calendar. A gully washer rain can be as damaging as no rain at all. A week of 100 degree temperatures and a wind at the wrong time can be devastating during the heading out time or the dough stage of the kernel in the head.

To me as a young farm boy, understanding these risks and the elements of nature came quickly. Watching the moist, blackening soil surface behind the farm implement was mesmerizing. A lazy dust-devil swirled over the crusty, untilled ground. Dust-devils resembled a miniature tornado as they swirled a cloud some fifty feet into the air. Sea gulls swarmed and dived to the freshly turned soil to pick up worms and wiggling insects as they were uncovered. Sea gulls in Kansas may sound unusual, but they migrated in the spring and nested around larger reservoirs. They were drawn to a field by a small dust cloud behind the tractor. They may have showed up only a few times each year, but were a welcomed sight. Sea gulls appeared in what seemed to be perfect moisture and growing times. Not too hot, not too dry, not too windy, not too cold, and not too wet!

The risks and gambles a farmer took were monumental, and harvest was the reward for a year's hard work and nurturing of the soil and seeds. Just like today, wheat was cut in June and early July. There were no cabs on the combine harvesters. The reel turning on the platform looked like a rotating wheel or the paddle powering a river boat. However, on the combine it was positioned in the front and rotated to pull in the crop that was cut at the surface by the back and forth motion of the sickle bar teeth. The sickle bar cut the straw below the seed head, which was pushed on the platform by the reel. These dried, golden sheathes of wheat were then funneled into the shaker header that moved the cut-off heads into the cylinder. The heads of the wheat were crushed and rocked as it worked its way through the shaker panels and the seed dropped to the bottom. The wheat seed accumulated into a lower pit channel and was augured to an elevator which lifted it to an overhead bin. Under ideal conditions, there were no grain heads or beards in the bin. Occasional grasshoppers or foreign materials such as sunflower heads or green weedy leaves made it to the collecting bin. A perfect field of golden wheat would have no weeds, no wet spots, and no water in the terrace bottoms. It would also have no wind and no triple digit temperatures. Perfection is hard to attain, but the few times that it happened brought a twinkle of pride to a farmer's eye and spirit. The term, a poor dirt farmer, could be taken two ways. It could refer to the low economic returns of the job of being a farmer, or it could refer to pity and hopelessness. The drive of a farmer and his trust and hope for a crop overcame any feeling of being poor. Farmers who felt sorry for themselves didn't last long.

After sitting on my father's lap and steering the red International 650 tractor, I soon advanced to standing on the side platform. Sitting on the fender over the huge, rotating, Goodyear tires gave me a bird's eye view of the power and work of the tractor and the field cultivator tilling the soil.

I would ask, "Can I drive?"

"Sure, crawl over here and I will help you learn," my proud father instructed.

These tractors had a hard metal foot clutch on the left forward base which was too stiff for a small farmer boy to push in and change the gear. But I soon got the knack of shifting the long pedestal shaft with the black knob on the top with the markings for the gear location. My dad pushed in the clutch with his foot, and I shoved the gear shift arm into the next position. The upper left gear notch was for very slow movement. Second, third, fourth, and reverse were easier to find the appropriate notches to slide the gear cogs into place than first gear. The smooth shifting and release of the foot clutch was essential to prevent a herky-jerky movement. Dad and I were a great, happy team.

"Daddy, when can I drive the tractor all by myself?" I begged.

"Be patient son," he answered. "About the time you learn to drive the tractor, you will not want to do it anymore."

The Ford tractor was smaller and we used it to cultivate the corn row crops. It was used to pull the mower and hay rake alfalfa. Sitting on the metal seat with a wire cushion, the farmer was exposed to dust, insects, and heat or cold, which were all just part of a day's work. Since the tractor was smaller, it seemed it was more manageable for me sitting on the lap of my beaming father. When I was seven years old, I was given my first solo field work pulling a hay rake. I am certain that I had proved I could handle the small foot clutch pedal and shift the easier gear handle. My dad mowed the alfalfa on a hot Saturday afternoon. After drying for two days, the hay needed to be raked into windrows so that it could be baled. It was Memorial Day and the hired man was given the holiday off. I was needed to pinch hit and drive the tractor for my dad. Having no doubt earned his trust, this farmer boy thought nothing of getting his first chance behind the wheel having just turned seven only a few weeks earlier.

Raking hay was a wonderful job because the side rolling tines of the rake placed all the hay to the left side in a windrow. Getting to the end of a long field, I turned around and reversed the direction to rake a second windrow, throwing it into the first windrow to make a larger, central row of the fragrant alfalfa. Balling up a large chunk at the end of the turnaround, or not getting the two rows together was forbidden. If a large chunk occurred, it required stopping the tractor and getting off to pull the intertwined mess of moist hay apart and redistributing it in the long, winding, meandering windrow line. By late afternoon, my dad's brother, Uncle Ivan, arrived to start the baling process. If I left any balls, it attracted his attention. He would have to get off the baler to separate the balls, which slowed him down. What was worse was that he reported that I was not doing the best job of raking to my dad. The art of mowing the alfalfa, drying it just enough that the leaves were still somewhat moist, and raking it gently so the leaves did not fall off the stem was the farmers goal to master. We always prided ourselves with making good, dry, and leafy hay. The cows loved the leaves, and it helped make the stalks tastier.

My dad was in the field next to me and was able to watch my every turn. He seemed to know that with the warm afternoon heat, dozing off was always a potential hazard. I took the responsibility seriously and did not want to jeopardize any future tractor driving. He walked over across the windrows, and I stopped the tractor to talk to him.

"How is it going, son?" he asked, his joy in seeing his tow-headed boy sitting in the driver's seat evident. "Does the hay seem dry enough?" he would ask.

"Yup, and I see what you mean about not turning around too sharply at the end and make it ball up," I replied.

"You're not sleepy, are you?" he asked with a voice warning that this was a possibility for even experienced tractor drivers.

"Nope," I would answer with the confidence of youth.

His parting words of advice were, "Well, be careful, and if you get tired, just stop the tractor and I will come over to relieve you."

Several years later, when raking hay, I ran over a nest of honey bees. They immediately attacked. I was their target, sitting up in the tractor seat. Throwing the gearshift into neutral, I leapt off to flee the mad honey bees. The swatting and instinctive running away seemed to infuriate them more. The bites on my neck—two on the face, and three more on my back from the stinging bees—were excruciatingly painful. The bite sites were soon welts the size of a silver dollar. The scene could have been worse, but for some unknown reason the swarm stopped pursuing me as I ran across the field. I had visions of Winnie the Pooh or bear scenes in books where the bees pursued the victim for miles. I limped back to the farm house. My mother the nurse took every medical emergency in stride and did not overly alarm the patient. She calmly took the tweezers and removed several of the stingers that were still protruding above the skin surface. She quickly placed a cold, wet dishtowel with ice compresses on the bite areas to help reduce the swelling. Very few things hurt more than a bee or hornet bite. The histamine release triggers a painful reaction, and area turns red and swells immediately. After the cold pack, Mother applied a baking soda poultice to the puffy welts.

We called up a neighbor who had honey bees for their garden and orchards. Maude Clark came with her beekeeper suit, complete with long sleeves. She wore a funny looking safari hat with a screen netting. She lured the bees up out of the hole in the alfalfa field and into a box-like contraption to transport them back to her hives. Bees and wasps were never again my friends.

Within a few hours, the tractor and farmer boy were back to work. Farm accidents, equipment breakdowns, or emergencies such as bees were all part of a farmer's daily life. Managing these mishaps and incidents was just a part of the day. The work still beckoned, and it all had to be done without whining.

 മ⊙ര

FARMER BOY GOES TO SCHOOL

My first day of school was fast approaching. Everyone asked questions that could be summed up as, "Are you excited to be going to school?" I was not excited at all. School changed the way I spent my days with my dad and our animals. We did not have kindergarten, and all eight grades were in a three-story brick building built in the early 1900s. The first grade was on the top floor, which had freshly gray-painted, shiny concrete steps. The wooden banisters had a new coat of varnish and everything sparkled.

The principal's office was at the top of the stairs and he was Dad's first cousin, Kenneth French. Having a relative as the principal did not pave the way for me. There were no favors given. I did not think he even knew who I was.

Mrs. Adams was an institution as the first-grade teacher. She was a formidable, middle-aged woman who had been married sometime along the way. Her print dresses were always secured around her middle with a one-inch-wide, shiny belt. A wide brown barrette secured her well-permed, wavy, graying hair tight against her head. Her eyes squinted and almost closed when she smiled. She wore matronly, black-laced, one inch, high-heeled shoes. She appeared kind and welcoming to a six-year-old. She was a disciplinarian, but not to the extent of paddling children. She sent students next door to the principal if any reprimands were needed. I envisioned corporal punishment as I carried my books into the hot and stuffy room on a bright warm September morning, but was relieved to find no dunce caps or paddles.

My school career, so to speak, got off to a rocky start even before the bell sent out its last call. I was walking between the individual flip-top desks with pedestal style swivel seats, looking for one with my name on it when trouble found me first.

My second cousin, Layton Irby, was already in his seat when he saw me approaching down the aisle. He was one of those ornery kids who never got caught doing anything wrong. He was small and very short and his cuteness exuded from an ever-present smile on his pudgy little cheeks. As I reached my desk, he nonchalantly stuck out his leg in the aisle to trip me. Quick to my wits, I saw the barricade and got down on my hands and knees to try to push his stubborn stiff leg back under his seat. Not aware of Mrs. Adams arrival in the room, I heard her bark out, "What are you doing, Jimmy?" Busted. Caught red-handed, I was sent to stand in the corner with my nose touching the wall before I even sat down and opened a grammar book.

Mrs. Adams would not hear one word of my explanation and acted as if she already had a premonition that I was a trouble-maker. Had my older brother, thirteen years before me, set me up? No way! I did not cry, but I surely wanted to after what seemed like an hour standing alone in the corner. I was finally sent back to my desk to try to refocus on this school stuff.

Those were the days when it was a known fact that if you got in trouble at school, you were in even more trouble at home. This hung over my head all day, even at recess and lunch in the cafeteria. Whether my sixth-grade sister found out, I was never to know, but being in such close quarters in a school house, news travels fast.

There was no way I was going to confess to my mom and dad. Upon getting home that first day, I quickly changed into my chore blue jeans and tee shirt and escaped out the back door. My mother may have sensed something, but she only asked, "Honey, how did your first day at school go? Did you like Mrs. Adams? You know she has had all four of you?" My answers must have passed muster, but I still suspected that Mom read some hesitancy in my responses.

That night, Uncle Ivan and my second-grade cousin came over to talk to my dad about borrowing a piece of farm equipment the next day. Alan was full of mischievous energy, always a bit hyperactive, always in motion. This night he was almost beside himself. I was sure he was about to blurt out, "How was standing in the corner today, Jimmy?" on several occasions, but his father pushed him back with his hand before the words could get out. I cowered behind a chair, just knowing he was going to rat on me. Finishing his business with my father, Uncle Ivan and Alan left by the back door. Whew! I had been saved for the time being.

How was it that wise parents seemed to sense the situation and know when to start the interrogation process?

"So, did everything go all right today, Jimmy?"

The tears erupted, and the details came pouring out. Bumbling and trying to catch my breath between the sobs, I tried to make my case. Surprisingly, this was one time they seemed to understand. Either I had done a rather good job of laying out my appeal, or they knew that Mrs. Adams was a no-nonsense teacher. Getting it off my chest made me feel as if an elephant had been removed. The ice cream at bedtime helped soothe over my feelings. I said my prayers with my mother and asked for help and guidance at school the next day.

Either my prayers were not answered, or I had not been sincere in my requests to God. However, the second day of school started off much better. That morning we started on our numbers and were introduced to our first *Dick and Jane* reading book. "Dick and Jane. Run, Dick, run. Jane run. Spot. Tip. Run Spot. Run Tip." It was repetitive, and recognizing the words and their patterns was a snap. Recess that morning on the swings, the big slippery slide, and the oversized teeter totter was great. Lunch at the cafeteria was seamless and the following noontime recess was relaxing and a confidence builder.

Hot and sweaty from the nonstop running and playing, we all ran back to the school and up the three flights of steps to the classroom. Whatever passes through a six-year-old's mind is a mystery. For some unknown reason, yet another cousin, David, picked up an eraser full of white chalk and hit Layton over the head, sending the flying powder everywhere. Sticking to his sweaty forehead, it was like powdered sugar dripping down his face. Before it was over, there were four of us popping the chalky erasers over one-another's heads. It was then that Mrs. Adams appeared in the room behind our backs. What could the old pro teacher have thought about these little hellions caught red-handed in their deviant actions?

"Stop it! Stop it! Stop it! You boys," she screamed. She then yelled in exasperation, "This conduct is not acceptable! Why in heaven's name did you think this could be done in school?" Since there were only three corners in this room, the three other villains each got their first corner reprimand. I, as a repeat offender, was sent into the coat closet for my penalty box. Once again, I had not started this foray, but was caught red-handed. Wow, two days in a row! This school thing was not starting off well. Run Tip Run, Dick and Jane, and the numbers thing was going well. Recess was a hit. But this standing in the corner thing set a bad precedent.

Something must have changed, or maybe it was the new seating arrangement. My desk was moved right up front, close enough to smell the perfume of Mrs. Adams. Though I thought my cousins were the real trouble makers, I liked being under the close, watchful eyes of the teacher. No more corners were in my future. I thrived in numbers, words, and the first grammar books.

My brother, who was now married and in his second year of college, came home to visit one weekend. Upon hearing of my rocky first days of school, he sputtered, "I always said Mrs. Adams was mean!" I never heard him coming to my defense in this way before and this helped soothe my feelings.

I went on to love Mrs. Adams and her strict classroom control. It was good that I accepted the system because I was to have her again the next year in second grade. This poor old teacher ended up with a combined class of first and second graders.

My mother was never critical of a teacher or of any of the teaching we were given. The next spring, Mrs. Adams came to our house one evening after school to see my mother about some church business. Mother was working in the flower garden, and Mrs. Adams rolled down her car window to visit with her. I ran into the house to bring out a heaping plate of freshly baked, chocolate chip cookies. With my two front teeth now missing, I lifted the plate up to Mrs. Adams as she chatted away. She took the whole plate and put it over in the passenger seat. I politely interrupted their conversation saying, "But Mrs. Adams, I didn't think you would take the whole plateful."

She quickly smiled and seemed chagrined that she had not really been paying attention when I handed her those warm cookies. "Oh, my goodness, of course not. Definitely. I'll just have this one on the top," she said as she handed back the heavy plate.

My mother did not say a word as she stood nearby leaning on the hoe. She had not been embarrassed that I had asked for the rest of the cookies back. In later years, she retold the incident with pride that I had stood up to Mrs. Adams on *my* expectations.

ഽⓒര

James Kenyon

BOOKS FOR BOYS

My brother Claude was a reader. He read books about Dick Tracy, mysteries, and western adventures. He read paperbacks while sitting on the milk stool, book opened on his lap, head in the cow's flank, all while his hands kept doing the milking thing.

I was thirteen years younger and often compared to my brother, my idol. Claude had lost his two front teeth playing football when he took a punt in the chops. A prosthetic plate with two ceramic false teeth corrected his smiling upper plate and provided a great trick. He could place his tongue into the roof of his mouth and push the plate forward. The two middle big incisors would quickly slide out about one inch, and then back when his tongue was retracted. Despite Claude's intellect, good looks, and magnetic personality, I was most impressed with his projecting teeth stunts. When we were in a restaurant or at a public meeting, he would nonchalantly stick out his teeth at some kid sitting next to us. By the time the astonished kid got his mother's attention, Claude's teeth were back in his mouth and he was innocently looking away. As the little brother, I admired and envied this antic.

Claude breezed through his school work: Latin, chemistry, physics, and English. There was nothing he could not accomplish. He sang in quartets, played the trombone, competed in every sport, and read books everywhere he went. I, the little brother, was cut from a different mold. I couldn't sit still long enough in the house to read a book. The outdoor farm duties were my calling. Mother wanted me to like reading and all the stimulation of the imagination that it offered an open mind.

When I immersed myself in baseball, baseball cards, and baseball statistics, Mother went to the county library to check out books for me to read. *The Babe Ruth Story*, books about Mickey Mantle, Lou Gehrig, *Stan Musial: The Man's Own Story*, Jessie Owens, and the Ted Williams story. I methodically read each page, gleaning every detail, statistic, and historical tidbit that each book offered. I was a very slow reader, but I could regurgitate the facts verbatim. I had no idea about speed reading or skimming and I generally thought of reading as too tedious and something that kept me from outside adventures.

Mother subscribed to magazines such as *Wee Wisdom* and *Boy's Life* for me. She hoped that these stories would expand my horizons and stimulate my thinking process. With the lights out in my room at bedtime, I used the flashlight under the covers to check these magazines off my list. There were stories of outside adventures and interesting collections of things city kids were doing. The content did not engross me unless it was about animals or fishing. I tried my best to honor my mother's wishes and plowed through each month's issues.

Mother thought there should be something that piqued my interest other than sports and farm animals. She bought plastic models and bird kits which needed assembling and painting. I completed the gold finch, scarlet tanager, oriole, cardinal, and blue jay. Mother thought I might be interested in model air planes. Many other kids were constructing and collecting the latest Air Force jet models. After putting the last decals on the gray plastic fuselages, the models went back in the box under my bed.

I am sure some of Mother's efforts helped me think a little beyond just being on a tractor or doing farm chores. The speed reading was never to be, but the love of reading slowly developed and nonfiction was the only style for me. History came easy as it was all about reality. Geography and the study of topography, nature, and ecology became my passions.

There was nothing like a school teacher to bring out the personality of a student. I had the middle-aged Mrs. Adams for first and second grades. My Aunt Barbara was my third-grade teacher; she encouraged oral presentations for her students. Memorization, recitation, and choral readings were also her tools for expanding the mind.

Miss Janet was a new, first-year teacher right out of Emporia State Teachers College. It was unheard of in our little rural community to have a new teacher come to our school, much less a single, pretty, and radiant lady. I entered fourth grade believing it was going to be great! I still had not been given the latitude of sitting in the back of the room, but I did not feel that sitting in the first row where I could smell the perfumes and powders of this gorgeous teacher was a penalty. She had my full attention, and I excelled, although my conduct grades on my report card were still checked in the "needs improvement" box. Entries for restlessness, annoying others, talking too much, and incomplete homework still filled more space than the boxes on the left side of the report card which now had actual letter grades, no more of the satisfactory check marks. I could read, knew my numbers, and could sit still long enough to learn.

Then it happened. After two glorious months of bliss, my fourth-grade teacher informed us that her special friend was visiting the class the next day. I literally loved Miss Janet. Surely she knew it by the way I smiled at her. I was kind and brought her flower bouquets from my mother's garden. The cosmos and zinnias on her desk, in fact, were from me.

I fretted overnight and went to school the next day to meet my competition. I hoped he would not measure up. After the before-school playground time, the bell called us all in from the swings, teeter totters, and slippery slide. We students lined up at the new water fountain before heading into the classroom. I wiped the excess water on my shirt sleeve as I glanced up to catch this image of a tall man in a dark suit ambling down the dim hallway. He walked with such confidence and turned directly into our classroom where he took a seat in the back of the room.

Miss Janet stood at her desk and called my name. "Jimmy, would you like to lead us in the Pledge of Allegiance?" she said with a smile. "Sure," I said and eagerly stepped forward. The class rose and looked toward the flag on the wall. The recitation of the pledge ensued. I noticed out of the corner of my eye that this man in uniform was standing too with his hand saluting instead of over his heart like the rest of us. "And with liberty and justice for all." We finished in unison before I took my seat.

Miss Janet, with her beautiful smile and radiant expression announced, "Class, I would like to introduce my fiancé, Ensign Bob Scheibe." Everyone turned to see this tall, handsome man in his Navy dress uniform standing to greet us. He had gold medals and ribbons accenting the pockets of his tapered jacket. He could have been General Eisenhower as far as I was concerned. He was tall, gracious, and exuded friendliness. I had been beat out by a better man. He was home on leave from the Philippines. We pulled down the wall maps and looked for these distant islands in the Pacific Ocean. I learned of the islands' significance; it had only been a little more than ten years since the end of the war, and the tragedies that occurred in the region were shared with the students that day.

My enthusiasm for school work was briefly curtailed, but I consoled myself with the fact that at least I had Miss Janet for the remainder of the year before she was married.

Mrs. Janet Scheibe and I exchanged Christmas cards for the next fifty-six years. In October 2015, I received a letter in her beautiful hand writing. She informed me that she was showing the signs of early Alzheimer's. The first few lines of the letter were perfectly Miss Janet. By the second paragraph, the lines were gradually slanting down the page diagonally to the right and the words were not as perfect. At the bottom of the page, in her perfect penmanship, were the final words. "God loves you and so do I. Miss Janet."

I quickly responded with two letters, but no reply was received. Miss Janet was fading away.

₧₨

RHODE ISLAND REDS

What do you have when you combine a boy, his dog, a red flyer wagon, and a crate of thirty dozen large, brown eggs? Every Saturday morning, rain or shine, year-round, I could be found selling the family produce door-to-door. In a rural community of less than 300 people, this was me, the farmer boy, with my first entrepreneurial venture. It was my contribution to the family farm.

In our case, the chicken came before the egg. Every February, my father ordered two boxes of day-old, Rhode Island Red baby chicks from a hatchery in eastern Kansas. They came by rail or, most often, by postal service. The delivery date was always marked on the family calendar. I would start the countdown awaiting their arrival in the same manner that most children looked forward to Christmas. Baby chicks hatched after a twenty-one-day incubation period. They were carefully placed in a low, square, pasteboard box with regularly spaced, one-half inch diameter holes all around the sides and top. There was a padded, straw-like mesh composite in the bottom of each of the quartered compartments. Twenty-five chicks fit snuggly per compartment. The box lid would be tied at right angles with a multicolored, braided cord. It looked like a present! Though it came without wrapping paper, no birthday gift could match its appearance.

The shipment arrived one day after the chicks were packaged. My dad and I made the five-minute trip to the post office to pick up the much-anticipated box. Peeping could be heard before the door to the post office was opened. Inside the post office, the bank of mail boxes, all numerically ordered with small dial combination locks on the front, stood between us and the glorious, cacophonous chorus behind in the mailroom.

Inez Irby, the postmaster, appeared at the checkout window. Her smile either meant she was thrilled that we had responded so quickly to her phone call, or that she was also warmed by the sweet peeping sounds that filled the post office.

Two large, square boxes were carried out to the pickup and put in the front seat next to the heater. My dog Tuffy and I jumped into the back of the truck and off we went for the short trip home. If there was an extreme chill in the air, we wrapped the boxes with blankets for the ride to the farm.

A small rectangular brooder house awaited the chick's arrival at home. It was a miniature structure about ten feet by twelve feet, and this tiny house had a wooden plank floor and a door with a casement window on each side. Inside, the gas lit hover welcomed the furry, yellow peeps. One by one, we scooped them into our hands and gently placed them under the hinged flaps around the four edges of the brooder. These flaps had a small, domed opening in the center reminiscent of the cartoon mouse-hole openings in a wall. This allowed the scurrying peeps to enter and exit at will. The inside of the brooder had a bank of gas jets with blue flame adjusted to 100 degrees Fahrenheit. A thermometer encased in a metal bracket on the side allowed my dad to easily read and regulate the temperature according to the outside conditions. He would read and reset the thermostat to reduce the temperature down by one degree each day. A ground corncob bedding covered the floor of the brooder to allow for comfortable resting. This was also very absorbent for the soon-arriving chick stools and waste.

Three foot-long, narrow feed trays held a special, baby chick feed. It was a greenish-colored granule and resembled the texture of the breakfast food called Grape Nuts. The aroma enticed me, though I did not believe the chicks were attracted because of the smell. In no time at all after being placed under the brooder, the chicks started venturing out of the openings at the corners or in the domed main portal. There was an arched, wire guard over the feeder so that, after a few days, the chicks could not get into the feeders and soil the contents. Since they had not eaten in almost two days after leaving the hatchery, it was imperative that they fill their little craws for nourishment. My dad set up a water jar that resembled a Mason jar inverted into a saucer to allow the water to seep into the plate. The chicks drank, gulp by gulp, throwing their heads back with beaks pointed to the ceiling. A glug-glug sound of air bubbles rising to the top of the jar caused by the air vacuum frightened them and they would flutter away. They soon became brave as the water vacuum and air bubble noise became routine.

My dad was a remarkable natural husbandry man. Of these two-hundred chicks, it was rare for one of them to die. He carried boiling water from the kitchen each morning to refill the waterers and clean the jars. I did not understand at the time that this method sterilized and kept the potential water contaminants and bacterial growth at bay.

I rushed home from school each day to change into my chore clothes—blue jeans, flannel shirt, and work boots. I first had to check on the baby chicks. One time, I accidentally stepped backward with my galoshes and crushed a little yellow fluff ball. I knew he was dead, but I carefully placed the flattened little body back under the brooder. Many times, I blurted my transgressions at the dinner table after agonizing during the whole meal to work up the courage to tell the truth. It was on such an occasion that I had to come clean to my parents that I had killed one of the chicks. I do not know why I was so apprehensive to tell the truth; the adults in my life seldom reacted with anger. I had an inner need to please my parents, so I cringed upon fessing up. My parents always seemed to understand that accidents happened. The relief of having this guilt off my heart was overwhelming.

So yes, to me, the chicken did come first, and their growth rate was incredible. In only a few weeks, these adorable peeps started to get pin feathers and the powdery, soft, yellow fluff blended in around their new, brownish-red feathers. They began to look like a patchwork quilt. The little yellow fuzz was soon gone, and a gangly, adolescent poult would run and jump through the brooder house. The young chickens flapped their wings with excitement and fluttered in and out of the brooder, chasing each other and playing. The brooder hover had a chain on a pulley at the top. My dad started to lift the hover each day as the chicks grew. Since the building had little insulation, this manipulation was essential for the life of these new chicks.

By the time they were four weeks old, the outside, south-facing door could be opened to let in the fresh spring air and sunshine. It was opened at first only a crack, then a brick-width, and eventually left completely open to the outside air. An old screen door was propped in place on its edge across the entrance to keep the young chicks inside. Dad kept a close watch on the weather or sudden wind shift so that he could close the door if needed. A corncob was put under the sliding windows to allow for ventilation. This kept the ammonia buildup from the chicks' waste deposits under control as it was neutralized by the circulating outside air.

By the first of April, the door could be opened wide and the screen slipped back to allow the chicks out into an enclosed, fenced-in, rectangular pen. Chicks running and flapping their adolescent wings was hilarious to watch. These new poults pecked at what seemed to be invisible specks in the dirt. This was the gravel that settled in their gizzards and allowed the chickens to grind their feed.

The gates to the outside pen were eventually opened. We had free-range chickens before the public understood the concept. The nearly 200 pullets and roosters were free to roam over the entire farmstead. They set off in groups of four to eight and explored the area. Scratching at the dirt was a favorite pastime. Chasing insects and grasshoppers with their necks outstretched in full running motion became quite a game. They were very brave, but a high-circling, soaring chicken hawk could strike terror. The chickens raced back to the brooder house for protection until the all-clear was given.

Young roosters grew a bright red comb on the top of their head and two velvety wattles under the chin region. Soon after, they started to learn to crow. Those first attempts were not unlike a pubescent boy with his voice changing. They stretched their necks skyward and made a garbled, croaking sound. The young roosters appeared to get up on their tiptoes. This must have been the physical position nature required for them to eventually call out their distinctive cock-a-doodle-doo. I could imitate their crowing and for the rest of my life was the featured wakeup call at church and 4-H camps, early morning rousting call at the college fraternity, or any other inappropriate time that might need a little crowing levity.

These same roosters were a staple for our dinner table. My mother dressed six to ten at a time from slaughter, scalding of the carcasses, feather plucking, and cutting up the pieces. Plucking wet chicken feathers was an art form. It will never leave my memory, nor will I ever yearn to do it again. Chicken was served at noon meals for the farm hands. The rest was frozen for our meat during the winter months. To this day, no chicken has ever tasted as good as those farm, free-range, Rhode Island Reds.

The pullets were moved to the larger hen house about the time they began laying eggs. The first several months that they started laying, the eggs were smaller with a slightly tapered end. These perfectly ovoid, brown eggs were almost too pretty to eat. Since they were smaller, they were not worth as much as the grade A, large, brown eggs. Each month, as the pullet grew into a yearling chicken, the eggs got larger. The quality of nutrition of their food along with exercise around the farmstead made for a very thick and hard shell.

There were hay stacks along the perimeter of the hen house and a nearby cow barn with a hayloft. Some of the chickens preferred to lay their eggs in a hidden nest or crevice rather than in the bank of nests along the wall in the hen house. Dad and I would spot a nest or a chicken wandering off to find her favorite secluded area in the hay mow. Spotting these nests was essential so that the eggs could be gathered every evening. If the nest was not found, the chicken went back each day to lay her egg. After ten or twelve days, she had enough eggs that she would sit on the nest, around the clock, for twenty-one days.

Occasionally, a possum, weasel or coyote preyed on these outlying nests and raided the eggs at night. Aiming a flashlight on a nest before reaching into it after dark and finding a hissing, prehistoric-looking possum's eyes reflecting back at me gave me the willies. Bull snakes sucking eggs in the nest was another hazard of nighttime egg collection. This was the reason hens were trained to lay their eggs in the hen house.

The phrase "coming home to roost" was so true. At the end of the day as the sun started to set, the hens headed back to their houses for the night. As one of my chores, I had to close the propped up, small hatch door in the evening. At times, when I got home late or had forgotten to close the hen house at dusk, I had to bravely trek out in the dark to close the door with the aid of a flashlight. Many times, the 150-yard trip in the pitch dark to close the forgotten chicken house door was followed by a world-record-shattering sprint back to the farmhouse. Every boogey man or demon that could be imagined chased me back to the house and the porch light. The many trees, shadows, and the wind made this dash even more daunting and spooky. No matter the age—six or sixteen—this frightening run back to the house was always scary. After I unexpectedly witnessed my own mother out of breath one night after going out to shut up the chicken house door, I realized I was not the only one afraid of the dark.

By the time I was six years old, gathering the eggs was one of my chores. Whether it was raining, snowing, or the ever-present Kansas wind blowing, the task had to be done each evening. The large, wooden, west door allowed access to the chicken house. The banks of nests were open to the front, and each nest in the row of twelve was about one foot square. The eye-level row of nests along the walls had oat straw liners. A two-inch lath extended along the front to keep the straw and eggs from rolling out. Some nests seemed to be more used as several eggs were nestled in them among the straw. I gathered the eggs in a pail—fifty, sixty, seventy, and sometimes up to 100 brown eggs. The chickens had to be watered, fed, and the straw bedding replaced in the nests. When leaving the hen house, the big west door was secured with the latch and a stick. It was amazing that predators were not more prevalent.

I learned by watching the hens that laying an egg was not a simple process. Some chickens were early morning layers and others got the urge at various times of the day. Usually it was a very routine, circadian rhythm routine as the hen would lay her egg at the same time each day. Observing them from above through the gabled, skylight windows and trying not to disturb their routine, I could see the hens begin to mosey and purposefully walk toward the awaiting nesting compartments. They could not actually fly, but with a hopping jump and flapping of the wings, they could make the three-foot leap with reasonable grace. Rarely did they miss, but if they fell short, they held on to the front board of the nest with the beak until the foot connected to propel them upward.

Seeing a hen leap into a nest, turn around, and adjust her positioning reminded me of a person lowering into a comfortable chair and maneuvering on the seat cushions before finally plopping down to rest. Some insisted on having the straw perfectly around and under their bottom sides. Others would lay their eggs on the bare, wooden nest bottom. They would sit contently for as long as half an hour before the egg moved down the oviduct and started to press against the vent opening. As a boy, I assumed that the tapered point of the egg, logically, came first. Alas, it was not true. It was the end that was more domed and oval that put pressure and slowly expanded the vent opening. Not unlike child birth, the egg slowly appeared and the moist surface helped it push through the opening as the hen rose up on her haunches to strain. The perfect, ceramic colored creation plopped into the straw. The steam coming from the egg in the colder days was not unlike my breath when the crisp morning air met my warm exhale.

Once the egg had dropped out of the hen, an instinctive reaction to jump and make a flying motion out of the nest occurred.

Flapping its wings several times as if to stretch and reflect on the moment, the hen started a routine cackling rhythm. This vocalization could go on for fifteen minutes, nonstop. Any farm kid learned to imitate this cackling, and I showed off this unremarkable talent to city kids, girlfriends, and family members. The tilt of the head with the face and eyes showing a whimsical twinkle, and the slow "baack, baack, baack" prelude, then a crescendo to the more rapid "baack, baack, boock, boock, boock" followed by a pause and repeat, over and over, was music to a farm boy's ear. Multiple hens cackling in their individual cadences was like a pond of bull frogs, each blending their own rhythms.

I learned that a chicken only laid one egg at a time. During the peak of laying season, which was called a clutch, a hen laid about five or six eggs each week. Some talented, prolific hens laid an egg every day for six months nonstop. The most productive hens could lay three hundred eggs in a year. They tapered off toward the end of the clutch and abruptly stopped laying altogether. This unproductive period was called the molt. The hen would back off her feed consumption, start losing her feathers, and often sit on her roost and seem to pout or sulk. She would go into a lethargic state, not wanting to move much. This molting coincided with the change of the length of daylight after the fall equinox. Sometimes the egg production from all the hens dropped dramatically. The physical nature of the hen house took on the signs of molting. There were dropped feathers everywhere and the mood seemed to take about six weeks up to two months to recover. From late October until February, the flocks' egg production declined to as few as one-fourth the normal numbers each day.

Double-yolk eggs were very uncommon, but once a hen laid one, she seemed to have more in her clutch. Inside the oviduct, two yolks (ova) dropped and were encircled by the enveloping shell. We had one hen that laid a double-yolker every other day. It always had an extra thick shell and even some scattered, sparkling calcium spots at various areas on the surface of the shell. Since watching all day to see which chicken hopped up into a nest to lay an egg was not the highest priority for a busy farm boy, I never figured out which of those dark-feathered Rhodies was the double-yolker queen.

One year my dad decided to experiment with another variety of chick and he ordered a white Leghorn variety. These little chicks looked the same and peeped the same, but by the time they started to get feathers, they were obviously a chicken of a different cut and color. They were flighty and had high-strung personalities. They were not the moderately plump and docile, gorgeously sheened Rhodie. I believe we only experimented with them one year. They supposedly laid more eggs—white ones, of course—but the Leghorn's smaller body and less meaty carcass was not as tasty as the Rhode Island Red.

Since we had a farmstead that included pigs, the chickens that roamed thought the feed dropped over the fence to the sow pen was better tasting than the ground mash fed to them in the chicken house. The corn or milo chop sow feed was of a different grind, and some brave hens flocked to it regularly. Sows normally just let the chickens peck away and eat alongside them. Occasionally, an irritated sow had enough and would throw her head sideways, causing the chicken to flutter a few steps away, much like a boxer trying to avoid a punch.

Every once in a while a more carnivorous, clever sow was quick enough to snatch one of the chickens in flight and chomp into a leg or wing. This would be the chicken's last foray into the sow pen. All that was left was a pile of feathers. After finding this remnant at the scene of the crime several days in a row, my dad would wait after feeding the sows to see just which one of the sows was committing chicken murder. Once she was detected, he caught her with a snare over the nose, and I held the snare while he punched two holes in each ear and attached an old car license plate with wire through the holes in the ear flaps. The tag dropped over the sow's face and eyes. This handcuffed her, in a sense, because when she attempted to catch another victim feasting in her pen or next to her snout, she had to flip the license plate up just to see the crafty hen. Thus, the chicken was forewarned and had time to jump away to safety. Just this warning noise from the metal tag gave the chicken enough time to flutter away and avoid an early death.

Baby chicks, pullets, crowing roosters, possums, bull snakes, and predator sows made me appreciate the joy of animals, production, and reproduction all in balance with nature.

ഔ

THE NEW PREACHER

Our town, Bogue, only had one church. It opened in 1913 and my Grandmother Belle was one of the leaders who helped get it started. It began as a community church, but soon affiliated with the Methodist. One of the benefits of having such connections was that the Methodist conference organization assigned a minister to this charge, as it was called. Methodism in America is traced back to John Wesley and George Whitefield and the church was known for its circuit riders. The preachers would ride horses across the countryside to visit their parishes and all of the small towns and villages. Since we were a small congregation in a small town, we tended to attract young ministers who were just getting started or older men near the last few years of ministry.

Gerald Martin was appointed to the Bogue-Zurich charge in 1953. Everyone called him The Reverend Martin or, most affectionately, just Jerry. He was one of those once-in-a-lifetime ministers who connected with his new town, congregation, and the surrounding countryside. Though the era of the circuit riders had passed, this young preacher came with his horse.

Reverend Martin had passions besides bringing people to God with riveting, deeply biblical preaching. He loved horses and baseball. This allowed him to connect with nearly everyone. He had a great sense of humor. He was loquacious and had a wonderful, cackling laugh that could be heard at any community gathering.

Our minister rode his stallion with the skill of Roy Rogers. He was always ready to help farmers or ranchers with their frequent cattle roundups. Every rancher needed to corral their cattle and sort or wean the calves at least twice each year. For spring roundups, calves were branded, castrated, and vaccinated. Jerry was not svelte by any means, and he always looked somewhat out of proportion in the saddle, being slightly paunchy and wearing his white Stetson, wide-brimmed cowboy hat. He looked like a city slicker in his khaki pants, snap-up cowboy shirt, and cowboy boots. The farmers never changed their attire for any particular work day, and Jerry stood out among the straw hats, overalls, and the few blue jeans and patterned shirts. Irish, his horse, had some hot blood in him, but was nearly a perfect western quarter horse in physique. Together they rode the flank of a herd of cattle, and their spectacular instincts and movements made even the orneriest cow succumb to their demands. Riding on the horizon with the morning sun rippling in layers, Reverend Martin could have been on the set of any John Wayne oater. This interaction with the farmers brought many to his Sunday church services. His love of people and life made the church congregation grow and prosper through his seven years as the Bogue minister.

On cattle round up day, my dad called in additional help from my uncles and my cousin, Leon. Cattle were always suspicious of strangers. They were used to my dad and me, but if anyone else rode in the pickup, the wise old cows cocked their heads, perked up their ears, and worried nervously. Working cattle took a calm, nonchalant demeanor in movement and planning.

Dad organized the work crew. "Okay, I am going to take the pickup out into the far pasture over that hill. I will throw out a few bales of hay to call up the herd. I'll honk the horn a few times to get their attention. After a few minutes, I want you, Jimmy, to bring Tony over that draw on the south over there," he said with a point and motion. "Jerry, you and Irish should hold back a short time to let Jimmy get on the south end, and then you come slowly up on the right flank," continued.

He instructed my uncles and Leon on where to stand with the plan to bring the whole herd to the other side of the creek. Then we forced the cattle across the water on the east. This put them in a perfect position to run into the funnel-shaped swing fence, directing them toward the corral and holding pens.

"Jerry, do you have any questions?" Dad asked. "Jimmy, I know you know what to do. Just stay out of sight until the cows are all drawn up to the hay I've thrown out. Tony will know what to do as he has done this many times. The main thing is don't yell too much and keep your movements slow to avoid spooking the lead cows. We want to get every calf this year. It is important that once they cross the creek, we all close in quickly to make sure they all hit the swing fence before the leaders get wise and turn around to run back at us."

Instinct and knowing cattle seemed to come as second nature to a great cattle man. Dad and I were always on the same page. Whether he was on Tony and I was on foot or the other way around, we could cut out a cow and calf pair from a herd and take them to a pen for doctoring without disturbing the whole herd. I didn't know how talented we were until, as an adult and as a veterinarian, I worked with farmers who didn't know "sickum" about cattle, their movements, or their nature. I don't believe it is something easily taught. Either you have it, or you don't.

"Okay, any questions?" Dad would ask. At times, I thought he gave our helpers too much credit for understanding the plan, but in the heat of action, no one ever got yelled at too much for being in the wrong spot or making stupid moves.

"Remember, there are two old breechy leader cows who will want to break back on us. That one with the stub horn and the brockle-faced one with the dark red neck are the ones to watch," he warned us. Of course, I knew which ones he meant, but to the average Joe white-faced, red-bodied, white-legged cattle all looked the same.

Most roundups had at least one or two calves that got on the wrong side of the fence and escaped. They were never the smallest calves, but the 400-pound size that bolted and ran like lightning. Without fail, a plan of letting a cow or two back to help lead the herd to the corral was usually successful. The hard work of sorting and processing the calves was a full day of work. On the farm, it seemed daylight was always burnin'.

The Reverend Martin and Irish were such a skilled pair. The silhouette of them galloping to the flank of the cattle herd was spectacular. Even though Irish was still a stallion, he didn't get aggressive with other horses. Jerry could rope while still in the saddle and nab a cow inside a cluster of cows. He would draw her nearer to the horse by easing Irish forward when the cow let up tension on the rope and holding firm while she was pulling. In no time, the cow succumbed and would be doctored or loaded into a trailer.

My dad was thrilled when the preacher man was available to help us. So many good stories and tales were shared of the adventures of the circuit rider and his horse.

ဆာૹ

PLAYING BASEBALL

The Reverend Martin introduced baseball to the young boys in town and the farm boys in the surrounding rural area. He introduced us to the many hops and bounces of a rawhide ball by lining up nearly a dozen boys around the infield. Soon every boy had his own mitt and ball. Pickup games of workup with a few players at bat and everyone else in the field were played on the school diamonds before and after school. Recesses became all about baseball. The game 500, where there was a batter who hit fly balls and grounders to the ten to fifteen other boys scattered in the outfield, became a constant pastime. The boys of Bogue packed after school and weekends with throwing and fielding balls. Since our ages varied from six to thirteen, all the boys had to play and choose sides in order to have two teams to compete in pickup games.

Favorite major league players and teams surfaced on every boy's horizon. Baseball cards were purchased at the grocery store with regularity. Every single card came with a pink square of bubble gum. The powdery sugar coating of the gum was addictive and boys quickly learned to blow bubbles. Putting multiple pieces of gum in the mouth and developing a chaw allowed for carefully formed, larger bubbles to be blown. These could be expanded carefully until they popped and covered the entire face. It was remarkable that the collapsed layer of pink sticky stuff could be peeled off the face and put back in the mouth for the next crafty, air-filled art form to follow.

There was no limit to how many pieces of gum could be added to the chaw. Somewhere between twenty and twenty-five squares was my maximum. At least, to still be able to open my mouth to chew and blow any kind of respectable bubble.

The side of our limestone barn had a square stone that worked perfectly as a batting strike zone. I used a tennis ball and pitched complete games with the ball making marks in the strike zone. The bounce back was fielded flawlessly by me, now the charging infielder, and fired side-armed to another adjacent limestone block. Another hand-eye contact practice was using a perfect stick or shovel handle to hit rocks for hours. Throwing the rock up with the left hand and swinging with both hands was a perfect pitching machine.

Trading baseball cards was a side business. I put complete major league teams of cards together. I memorized every player's statistics, trade information, previous teams, and hometowns. I knew what year a player hit a specific number of home runs and his batting average. I knew every pitcher's earned run average and win-loss record by the year and career. I listened to the St. Louis Cardinals and Harry Caray's broadcasts on my brother's hand-me-down radio every night. I went to sleep with the radio turned in my window to pick up the clearest reception on station KMOX in St. Louis, some 600 miles away. It was an easy thing for me to remember and regurgitate these statistics. I never learned if this skill was marketable, but it has given me some seven decades of baseball minutia enjoyment.

I was the smallest boy on a team that was formed to travel to play games out of town. Coach Martin would say, "Tonight it will be Jimmy leading off and playing right field. Steve, you are at shortstop and batting second. Alan, you are at first and batting third. David, you're pitching again and batting cleanup." He proceeded on down the lineup with all nine starters. "Remember, this pitcher is wild and I think we can get him frustrated. Okay, let's get some ducks on the pond and get some runs. Jimmy, try to work them for a walk so that we get someone on to move them around." Coach barked out instructions from the third base coaching box while we batted. When we were in the field, he was constantly chattering and repositioning us to maximize our skills. We each realized that it took all nine players to be involved and work together if we were to overcome our size and the disadvantages we may have had against the bigger players from the larger towns. Our bench chatter, "here batter, batter, batter," or, "the pitcher's got a rag arm," became our common vernacular.

Since I was the lead-off batter, I had a method to reaching first base. An opposing pitcher always had difficulty throwing to a short batter as the strike zone was even smaller. I would crouch down and lean forward in the batter's box, making the target almost impossibly small for the young hurler. Walking became my ticket to get on first base. Choking up on the 28-inch bat helped me get around on a fastball, though leaving the bat on my shoulder and not ever swinging seemed to be the surest way to get a free pass with four balls. Right field was usually where a team buried or hid their weakest fielder and arm. Swatting mosquitos and hoping the ball wasn't hit to me became equally important. With each game and year of growth, I soon developed into an infielder, catcher, and pitcher with great range and accuracy. The fear of a fastball was eventually overcome, and being able to play against some of the bigger teams and players was a lesson for life in practice and perseverance.

Coach Jerry Martin didn't just bring baseball to town, he instilled in each of us a love of a game where overcoming barriers and difficult times was possible with practice. We never won more than we lost, but we were all winners. No trophy or ribbon could have replaced the valuable lessons and skills we learned. No one made it to the majors, or even played minor league ball, but in our minds, we could have played with the best of them at Fenway or Yankee Stadium. This was the era of the "Boys of Summer" and the great Milwaukee Braves—Aaron, Matthews, Burdette, and Spawn. Of course, Mickey Mantle and the ever-dominant Yankees were the favorites of most. I held out for Stan "The Man" Musial and the slumping Cardinals. They were our heroes, and we lived a vivid life vicariously.

🙴🙵

James Kenyon

THE REVIVAL

During the 1950s, the United States Bureau of Reclamation was charged with building dams across the country. Many of these dams were constructed for flood control. A few were for hydroelectric power. Others, ultimately, were used for the irrigation of cropland. Behind these dams, large reservoirs held back the water. Thanks to these dams, recreational fishing and boating came to rural areas. Many such reservoirs displaced low lying towns in the way. Such was the demise of the town of Webster when the dam was constructed across the South Solomon River some twenty miles downriver from our farm.

The South Solomon ran just north of us. My uncles had land that was adjacent to the river. Cottonwood trees propagated near these streams. These trees squelched the little water that normally flowed in the stream. There were natural springs that bubbled out in a steady flow of water. An occasional hard rain, a gully washer, filled the creeks and rivers. Webster Dam was constructed in 1955 and 1956. The huge flood gates were closed on May 3, 1956. The Corps of Engineers estimated it would take two years before the reservoir was full. They had not consulted with Mother Nature in their prediction. One of those notorious, gully washing rains occurred and within two weeks the water was running over the flood spillway gates at Webster.

In preparation for the construction of the dam, the dirt road past our farm was elevated and a sand-gravel overlay spread on the road surface. The grader ditches were cleared of weeds and brush as the elevators augured the dirt up to make a higher roadway. When the summer rains came, the water stood in the lower areas. Frogs would find this water overnight. The frogs left behind eggs that turned into thousands of tadpoles. As the water started to recede with evaporation, the tadpoles were concentrated. The water surface seemed to boil with their movement. Throwing some wheat, milo, or even a leftover sandwich into the water drove them into a fury.

In order to save them from drying up and shriveling to death as the water ebbed away, I took feed buckets and a scoop shovel to the rescue. These little inch-long pollywogs were poured into the cattle stock water tank. A log was also placed in the tank. When the little swimmers started to morph and lose their tails and get legs, they crawled up onto the floating log. In a few days, they were able to jump out of the tank to freedom. Watching them become frogs was a daily marvel.

Once the roadwork was complete, a steady stream of heavy rock trucks started roaring from the west delivering riprap boulders for the construction of the dam. From dawn to dusk these trucks downshifted and backfired as they slowed for the upcoming stop sign. The dust from their wheels rolled and clouded the area. Dust sifted into any closed window or door. Hanging clothes on the clothes line became impossible. Smelling the silt along my bedroom window had to be similar to what was a daily experience during the dust bowl years of the 1930s. Some think you have to find gold or oil to make it rich. I learned that to own a hill or butte that had sandstone for making dams was another way of striking it rich. The Hocker rock quarry thrived, and the families who owned it became wealthy.

This new reservoir attracted a marina, a state park with camp grounds, wildlife, and some bait shops. Perched on the chalk hills among the mixed prairie grass filled with meadowlarks and red tailed hawks, a tent was set up each summer. The area Methodist congregations held weeklong revivals complete with evangelist ministers and spiritual quartets. Every night the services attracted hundreds from the surrounding towns and countryside. My parents took me to every service. Songs such as "Just as I Am," "Just a Closer Walk with Me," and "Abide with Me" became ingrained in my memory. Bible study groups were held during the daytime for those camping and some of the families close to the area.

A choir of farm men and women was organized to lead the congregation. I was enthralled by the men who sang bass. Their booming voices seemed to fill the tent with a riveting vibration. It didn't seem possible that these men with their farmer's tans and slicked-down hair could put out such deep, beautiful sounds. The sopranos got attention, too. Often, a few warbling ladies would over-sing and belt out high notes. I had no idea what a tenor or alto was at the time, but they seemed to be hidden by the low and high singers.

An altar call occurred every night toward the end of the service. It seemed to me that those who were in attendance must surely have been saved before, or they wouldn't have been there in the first place. It would be years before I heard the term "born again." The ones who came to the altar and kneeled in prayer must have fit this bill.

Every year during the revival, a nasty thunderstorm rolled through during a service. The men hastened with activity, untying the canvas side flaps from overhead and tying them down to the anchor stakes. The wind whipped and a downpour would attack so violently that a prayer from the preacher ensued. The tent, miraculously, was never blown away. If the downpour was sustained, water quickly built up on the swooping, sagging top-panels of the tent.

I learned a lesson from an elder who said, "Do not touch the sagging tent panel with your finger—it will cause the tent to leak where the finger touches!" Of course, this was just like the Garden of Eden story. Many a boy had to see if touching could, indeed, cause leaks. Sometimes, the forbidden fruit was just too tempting.

I never quite appreciated the passionate pastor who had the altar calls. "This is the last verse of 'Just As I Am' that we will be singing. I call you to release yourself and come forward and accept Jesus!" he pled to the tent congregation. It sure seemed that we would sing that last verse just one more time for another half hour, at least.

Had it not been for the government building dams, I may never have known rock trucks, tadpoles, and tent revivals. "Just as I Am" will never be the same as it was under the gigantic white canvas tent with the sun tucking under the west horizon.

$\wp\!\infty\!\wp$

TUFFY THE COW DOG

Kenny Martin, the preacher's son, had a little black and white rat terrier that was going to have puppies. Since that Sunday night raid and the demise of Jack, I had been without a dog. Kenny, a chubby kid, was three years younger than me. I needed a puppy and this unplanned pregnancy fit the bill. So Kenny and I made a deal and I gave him fifty cents for one of the puppies.

Kenny's terrier, Trixie, had met up with Gladys Van Loenen's dog that lived on an adjacent street. He was an off-white, stocky dog with tan ears and a bobbed tail. Gladys had brought him to town when she married the widower farmer, Henry. I wasn't much concerned about pedigrees, but if I had to pinpoint the father dog's breed, I would say he was in the Staffordshire terrier or pit bull alignment of some sort. He was built like a middle linebacker. He was a lazy house dog, most of the time and a real couch potato. Evidently, when Mother Nature called, he had slipped out the back door and met Trixie in the dark alley. I had no concept of the actual deed; I just knew it took a meeting of some sort to have puppies.

When Kenny started showing up with money in his pockets, his mother, Luella, became alarmed. Was he stealing from somewhere? At bedtime she confronted him and put him on the hot seat. He finally broke down and tearfully admitted that he had been selling Trixie's puppies. One big problem was that she was just pregnant, as he had been told. He had to give my fifty-cent piece back, but I was promised the pick of the litter. Trixie couldn't have weighed more than eight pounds, even with a belly full of pups.

Finally, the day came when Kenny informed me at school that Trixie had her puppies the night before. He and I slipped behind the bus barn at the noon recess to run to his house a block away. We peeked in on the nursing mommy and three wiggling babies. I handed him the fifty-cent piece that I had been saving for the occasion.

I stopped after school regularly to watch the little mother and her growing brood. I believed there was nothing cuter than a litter of puppies. When their eyes opened near day twelve, their personalities started to materialize. Fat and plump, they waddled before learning to walk. Trixie was a wonderful mother and seemed to let them nurse all the time. I had my eyes on the black and white one. It was the most active and gregarious of the litter. It just happened to be a boy, but the sex did not matter to me.

The parsonage was next to the church. It was easy to check in on my purchase on Sunday mornings after Sunday school. I took my dad to see the pups. His approval was important to me and I could see he was smitten by the litter of puppies, too. The new life of any baby animal gave us both a thrill.

Six weeks to the day after they were born, I was able to pick up my puppy and bring him home. After the longest school day on record, I ran to Kenny's house. There on the back porch was his family and Trixie with her family of three. Kenny picked up the roly-poly puppy and handed him to me as tears rolled down his flushed and pudgy cheeks. I kept my excitement at bay as I could see this parting with such a loveable little creature was crushing to Kenny.

Trixie, too, couldn't quite understand why I was holding her pup. She became downright unhappy when I began to walk away with it. Her whining and jumping protest made the parting even sadder. I carried my yet-to-be-named purchase out the back door. Down the alley, we walked home to our farm some fifteen minutes away. Setting my pup down in the tall, lush, springtime grass at our farm border, I finally realized that he was actually mine.

It was a picture-perfect afternoon. The grass and nearby wheat field had thrived in the April showers and longer, sunny days. I was tired and sweaty from carrying my new dog. When I sat him down in the succulent greenery, he started bounding over the grass. It was taller than he was. He was not going to let me out of his sight, and his determination to keep pace with me caused me to say, "Why you little tuffy. You are some puppy!" The name Tuffy stuck, and no other was ever considered.

Tuffy was given a bed in the milk room of the limestone cow barn. A cardboard box was cut down and the top removed. One of my mother's old pink blankets with the soft satin fringe was tucked in to the bottom for padding. Tuffy had a distinct whimper that sounded like a moaning whine. I quickly mimicked the cadence of "un un un unnnaaah, un un un unnaaah." It sounded so pitifully lonely. My puppy demanded to be held and comforted. That first night, I took him with me to do my chores. Between tagging along and being carried, we gathered the eggs. His eyes lit up when he saw the chickens. I could still hold the fat little butterball. I would set him down and he bounded after me to catch up. I was amazed with his stamina and determination. The little black and white dynamo never seemed to tire.

"Un, un, unnnaaah," he called as I left him alone in the homemade box that night. I could hear him crying after I shut the milk house door. A puppy always spends the first night away from its mother and litter mates crying. I knew it was not possible to bring him into our farmhouse. At least fifty yards separated our house and the cow barn.

I worried all night about him being lonely. In future years as a veterinarian, I would imitate this little cry of "un, un, unnnaaah." Puppies immediately tilted their heads and knew that I could speak their language.

After this first long night, I put on my cowboy boots at the crack of dawn and rushed out to the barn to meet Tuffy. Upon opening the milk room door, I was greeted with "un, un, unnnaaah." Tuffy stood on his back feet with front paws on the edge of the box. His head peered over, as if to say, "it's about time you got here!" We hugged each other. His tough, wet, pink tongue cleaned my face from ear to ear. What a licker he had! His puppy breath had a musky fragrance. The cats started weaving between my legs and feet as they begged to be fed. They demanded their share of the attention.

Every farm has cats that live off mice and small rodents. Our cats were mostly tame, but occasionally a stray, feral cat started coming around to eat. I thrived in taming and domesticating any cat that came around. We always poured milk in pans after spinning off the cream in the electric Babcock separator. Tuffy loved the cats too. He let them eat from the same bowl, drink from his water pan, and curl up with him to keep warm.

"Un, un, unnnaaah," I called each morning, running to the barn. I turned the stiff, round knob and gently kicked the bottom of the swollen wooden door until it opened inward. I happily greeted Tuffy. Lifting him, he licked my face with his ever-present puppy breath. Tuffy and I were off for our day's adventures and work. We were best friends and inseparable in all our activities.

Our family's garden was fenced in with vertical stakes nailed to ten-foot, horizontal panels. There was a one-inch gap between each of the upright stakes. Tuffy ran around the outside of the garden until he found the hinged, swinging gate ajar. He thought it a great game to dig alongside me as I hand-weeded along the rows of carrots, beets, peas, onions, beans, and lettuce. His front paws worked furiously when he found an open spot to dig. The dirt missiles shot behind him through his back legs and became a heaping mound. He never disturbed any of the garden greens, but only dug in open spaces among the melon and the cucumber hills. He imitated my efforts as I progressed down the rows of plants. Tuffy learned this technique as a puppy and helped in this way all of his life. After a small divot was dug, he would lay down in the hole in the cooler earth, placing his head down on his paws and rear end up in the air with his stubby tail wagging with excitement. I threw him an earthworm and he caught it midair. Tuffy continued to flip the worm with his nose. He would tease it, roll it in the dirt, and when it stopped moving and the game became boring, he'd swallow in one gulp, just like a man devouring a raw oyster.

Each night, Tuffy was relegated back to his bed in the barn. He soon could scale the sides of the cardboard box. I cut down one side to make an entrance at ground level. New boxes were used as he grew. He chewed and decimated the boxes as he awaited my morning wakeup calls.

When school was finally out in May, we spent whole days together. His short little legs propelled him along behind me as I rode my bike. He was a Tuffy in every sense of the word. Unlike poor old Jack, his predecessor, my new dog was very, very smart.

Going to the cattle up north in the summer pastures was routine as I helped my dad each day. Tuffy circled with excitement as the blue Chevy pickup came up the driveway. He quickly learned that this meant a road trip. I lifted him into the front seat until he was old enough to gracefully jump from the ground to the bench seat with perfection. He manned the middle of the seat only briefly. On the very first pickup ride, he learned that he could not see over the dashboard. He immediately hopped onto my lap and reached up to the side window, poked his head out, and let the passing wind rush to his face. Squinting his eyes, his ears blown backward, his mouth open, and his tongue flapping with saliva, Tuffy dripped, yapped, and barked with excitement as we drove away for our cattle trip.

ജറ

James Kenyon

THE MANY TALENTS OF TUFFY

Tuffy the Ball Player: From his first days, Tuffy was infatuated with balls. A red rubber ball was his first toy. He carried it around and dropped it at my feet so I could throw it. Like a shot out of a cannon, he would turn in midstride and dart to where the ball was about to come down. He had an uncanny ability of anticipating how far and how hard I had thrown the projectile. After only one bounce, Tuffy leapt and caught the ball in the air. Like carrying home a treasure, he rushed it back to me and dropped it at my feet for a repeat performance. He crouched down in shortstop stance, panted, and rocked back and forth, awaiting the next ball to be hit or tossed his way. This game went on indefinitely as he never seemed to tire. If I had owned a Frisbee, Tuffy would have been equal to any Australian shepherd in competition today.

My dog was built like a sweaty, middle-weight wrestler, though he weighed only forty pounds. After rubber ball retrievals, he progressed to tennis balls, baseballs, large softballs, rocks, dirt clods, and even horse apples (a barnyard term for perfectly round horse manure droppings). Tuffy could catch them in midair. Rocks caused his tongue and teeth to bleed, but he never once complained and brought any and everything I threw back to me. It was I who insisted we take a break for a drink and petting. He loved it when I patted him hard on both sides of his chest while he stood with his front feet up to my waist.

To cool down, Tuffy would find a mud puddle to run through and stand in. He could dive into the stock tank and swim to the other side and back to get cooled off. Then he jumped out, gave a few vigorous shakes, and was refreshed and ready for our next venture.

Tuffy the Work Dog: The cows on our farm knew that Tuffy was as skilled as any blue heeler with inbred instincts to herd. My dog knew when to creep forward and nip at their heels. He had a deft ability to anticipate the cow's kick, much like a boxer ducking a punch. The cow would half run and always looked around nervously, worrying where Tuffy was positioned next. If he could have managed the gates, he probably could have been trained to bring home the milk cows from the pasture or wheat grazing fields across the road without us.

Tuffy the Hunter: We lived about a mile away from the slow, meandering Wild Horse. I never heard it referred to as a river, creek, or even a stream. It was simply called Wildhorse. Usually it was about one-inch deep. On most Sunday afternoons, I took my dad's .22 rifle and headed for Wild Horse. I would shoot at anything along the way that seemed like a reasonable target. Beer cans, pop cans, plastic bottles, or corn stalks set up on fence posts were often willing victims.

The railroad track was on the north side of our land and it headed west toward Wild Horse. Along the track was a telegraph wire that could be seen bobbing along the tracks toward the distant horizon. The blue-green insulators attaching the wire to the tee-shaped posts were vulnerable targets for this obsessed young hunter. The glass spraying was easy confirmation that the bullet had hit its target. On these hunts, Tuffy was always in the lead. He would freeze on point with only his stubbly tail vibrating in the air as he scouted every thicket or tumbleweed patch. Darting beneath the grass thickets, he chased rabbits, mice, and kangaroo rats.

The railroad bridge over Wild Horse was low and stretched across the little stream and wide sand bars on either side of the water. Make-believe train robberies, bridge explosions, or hair-raising leaps from a burning, fast-moving passenger rail car were acted out during these boy and dog ventures.

At Wild Horse, Tuffy chased the darting minnows as they jettisoned against the flow of the lazy stream. I often brought a bucket from home on these river hikes. Tuffy would dig in the sand to cool himself in the divot. These made perfect holes where I could divert the water off from the main stream and create small dams. Building sand levees would send minnows to these ponds before the water overflowed its banks. Cupping my hands, I could scoop them and splash them into the clean water in the bucket. Carrying the five-gallon bucket was a task with it half full of water and the day's catch. One hundred steps ... one minute rest ... one hundred steps ... one minute rest ... one hundred steps. Before long, the bucket, the farmer boy, and his best friend arrived at the cow tank at home. The minnows lived, swam, and thrived with the tadpoles and other small water bugs that happened to be scurrying under water. My dad did not seem to mind my relocation of any swimming creature, and neither did the cows or our horse, Tony.

Tuffy the Guard Dog: No one came to our house without Tuffy being on guard. He did not lay out the welcome mat. He would not growl, but instead put on a quivering, turned-up lip, raised the hackles on his back, and used piercing eye contact to warn any stranger on our farmstead. My uncles, farm hands, and the neighbors who knew him always talked to him and kneeled to greet him before proceeding on into the house or down to the barn to see my dad. They all knew he would bite at the heels of an unwanted visitor. They were leery of moving too fast or too far into the farmstead without making contact with one of us.

Tuffy the Kids' Dog: My oldest sister Janie had three boys who came on holidays from Texas. They came every summer for a month to visit and live with us. They were four, six, and eight years younger than me. Though I was their uncle, we behaved like brothers. Each of them would throw anything that wasn't tied down, and Tuffy played the game and retrieved it.

Tuffy the Loyal Homebody: Tuffy never strayed away from home. One evening, I heard a dog screaming in the distance and a car speeding, screeching, and speeding again. I ran down to the cattle pen and climbed up on a tall corner post. What I saw was a horrific sight in the distance toward town. Mean, hooligan high school boys had caught a stray dog and tied a rope around its neck and were pulling him behind their souped-up hot rod. About the time the poor helpless creature got to its feet, they would screech out and throw sand and dirt as the car careened off again at high speed. The scene and the crying would never leave my mind. I worried that they might do the same to Tuffy if they ever caught him straying toward town. But Tuffy knew where his home was and never strayed from it.

Tuffy lived a wonderful life. I hugged him as I left for college ten years later. When I came home on break, he was not there. I never asked, nor was it ever mentioned, what had happened to my dog. I knew that accidents on a farm could take a tragic spin. That dog made an indelible mark on my life. Even sixty years later, our family still tells stories of Tuffy, my best boyhood friend. I can still envision him chasing balls, herding cattle, and riding shotgun in our blue Chevy truck.

It is said that in one's life, if you can count on one hand the true friends that you have, you are one lucky person. I would include that if a boy or man can have one good dog, one good horse, and one good wife (in that order) he was one lucky man. God had blessed this man and he was a success in his life.

∞℘

THE RED WAGON

I pulled the Red Racer Wagon from the barn to the back-porch door. It was the best designed wagon I had ever seen (and have seen to this day). Santa Claus brought it to me for Christmas. It had sideboards all the way around. Each sideboard had two pegs that slipped down into slots on the lateral edge of the rim. It looked much like our stock and grain truck. My red wagon was my way of hauling product on the farm. It was in constant use. Whether it was full of roasting ears of corn neatly stacked from the front to the back, stuffed with chicken manure from cleaning out the hen house, rattling with rocks, or loaded for the weekly egg route, my wagon was in constant use.

Every Saturday morning, beginning when I was seven, I placed the egg crate in the red wagon. Tuffy knew the routine and the egg route well. When the wagon came out of the cow barn parlor, Tuffy knew his morning as the protector of the egg wagon was about to begin.

My route was usually the same. We lived on the outskirts of town and it was only a ten-minute walk to our closest neighbor. It was a safe and easy trek for a seven-year-old, his dog, and the little red wagon. My village of Bogue had a population of 300. I knew everyone and every house in town. My customers depended on me to stop and they had their egg cartons ready. I took the eggs from my layered crate and filled each carton along the way. There were times when I stopped by a new house and tried to get the housewife thinking about if they wanted to start buying eggs from me.

The first stop on my egg route was always Rosie Ashcraft's. She was a pretty, strawberry-blonde woman with the most freckles I had ever seen before or since. Her beautiful smile and personality always started the delivery route on a good note. Whether it was one or two dozen, she always had an order for me. I envied her children, Mike and Cheryl, because they were still in their pajamas and watching TV cartoons as I counted back change to their mother.

Eggs were twenty-five cents a dozen in those first few years of my route. Over the next seven years, the price was raised to thirty-five cents per dozen. Being able to multiply in my head by thirty-five became so easy. In the classroom, I earned a reputation for being able to answer multiplications for 70, 105, 140, 175, and 210 without even having to think about it.

The next house was Mrs. Gosselin. She had seven children and her husband had been tragically handicapped in a car accident. Having such a large family with only her income, Mrs. Gosselin seldom bought many of my large brown eggs. The next door was Grandma Tripplet. She bought one dozen eggs every other week as regular as clockwork. Then it was on down the street to Gladys VanLoenen, Mrs. Radcliff, Nina Elliott, Louella Martin, Vi Thompson, Roma Lee Irby, Virginia Hooper, Maude Clark, Phillis Olsen, Grandma Johnson, Belva Stevens, Marie Thompson, Millie Young, Arva Green, Aunt Mary, Sandy Thompson, Liz Van Loenen, Noretta Clayton, Vera Fabricus, and finally, Leona Irby. Leona had at least nine kids, so her five to six dozen eggs order was always the largest and usually finished off my supply. As the route grew, I added another, smaller crate to the back of the wagon to meet the demand.

Tuffy hunkered down under the wagon when I was making the delivery and knocking on doors. He was a good business partner, though he growled and was a heel biter. If someone came close to my wagon while I was not with him, he warned them with a snarl and crept a few steps toward them. He had a reputation all over town as a dog to leave alone. No one came close to my wagon or my dad's pickup truck. I loved Tuffy, and I knew he loved me. I reveled in the fact that he could whip any dog in town. That was a thing of pride for boys, to have the best and toughest dog. If there was ever a dog that challenged Tuffy, it only happened once.

If I had not sold the whole case and a half of eggs by the end of my route, I delivered them to the local grocery store. The grocer, Tom Tripplet, bought the remaining eggs and stored them in his walk-in cooler. Parting the long, plastic strips hanging vertically over the entrance to the cooler was fun. It was an instant, cooling relief after the walking the egg route. I never knew where the eggs went, but they were not sold in the store. Other farmers also brought in their extras, and eggs at these rural collection sites were picked up to be moved to the cities.

The money from the eggs was brought back home and given to my mother. I took out five cents to buy baseball cards. Occasionally, another nickel bought a Big Boogie or Black Cow candy bar. The balance of the money became my mother's. In those times, for our family, it supplemented our monthly grocery bill. Mother had a charge account at the grocery store. Our monthly food costs came to about $70 in those days.

The red wagon was also used for pop bottles that I collected from the grader ditches. There was no such thing as recycling to be encouraged. As people drank a soda while driving, the empty bottles were typically thrown out the window. I came to the Earth Day scene early as I collected these empties along the roadsides. My dad would stop the tractor when he was moving from one field to another on the roadway and pick up a discarded pop bottle. I sat in the pickup with my eyes to the ditches when we drove daily to deliver feed to our cattle at the pastures some seven miles north of town. Fall and winter were the best times to spot these bottles in the brown, dried ditches. Green bottles were the easiest. 7-up, Bubble Up, Teem, and Squirt were always green, and I was too naive to know that these were beverages very commonly used for mixing drinks. Drinking and driving was very common. Following prohibition and the return of the servicemen from WWII, it was a big time for liquor consumption, fast driving, and the natural consequence of auto fatalities.

I collected pop bottles until I had one-hundred of them. The bottles were worth two cents each. I delivered them to the same grocery store for redemption that bought my eggs. I wanted an even number of bottles so that I could get two crisp dollar bills for this recycling endeavor. Along with my twenty-five cents per week allowance, this money was put in my savings account at the bank. With the brown, varnished, wood-grained side boards on the wagon, Tuffy and I pulled it the five blocks to the store about every three months.

⬥⬥⬥

THE FERTILIZER

BUSINESS

The growing chickens in the brooder house had ample accumulations of manure in their bedding and the chicken house had to be cleaned periodically. One of my chores included loading the manure and corncob bedding into a wheel barrow. I pushed the loaded barrow out into the cornfield and emptied the contents. It took many trips to deliver the manure. I thought surely there should be an easier way, or at least a monetary return for this chore. My red wagon was about to come in handy again.

I hatched an idea. What if there were a market for this high-grade fertilizer? With my Tom Sawyer mindset, I coerced the Gosselin boys into bringing their wagons to our farm. With three wagons loaded to the rims with chicken manure, we headed off to town. We were convinced we could sell this much-needed commodity for any backyard garden. We knocked on door after door asking the housewives if they needed any garden fertilizer. After what seemed to be several dozen "no interest" replies, one of my egg customers bought all three loads for twenty-five cents each. We spread the manure in her garden and raked it evenly, hoping that this great fertilizer was not too high in nitrogen. The last thing we wanted was to burn up Mrs. Thompson's tomato plants and get a bad reputation. We pulled the wagons back home and proceeded to clean the chicken house. Since our great idea had not been accepted with rousing enthusiasm by the housewives of Bogue, we used the wagons to take the remaining manure to the corn fields. Though it was

79

helpful to me to have my friends in an assembly line cleaning the chicken house, it was the last time I coaxed the Gosselins into such a money-making exercise.

Once the chicken house was cleaned out, new oat straw was evenly scattered on the board floor. The chickens scratched and pecked away at the oats remaining in bearded heads. With both feet rapidly scratching away, it looked as if this was a drug induced activity. Seeing the chickens so happy and excited for the new bedding was one of the rewards of having a clean chicken house. The pullets seemed to appreciate the new bedding, and I felt sure the removal of the ammonia-filled scat made the new oat scent much more refreshing.

So whether it was with eggs, pop bottles, or manure—the little red wagon, Tuffy, and I made many trips to town. Though the income and money raised was important for our family, these times of knocking on doors, looking at people in the eyes and asking for their business was probably more valuable for my development than the monetary reward.

ഇറ

TONSILLECTOMY?

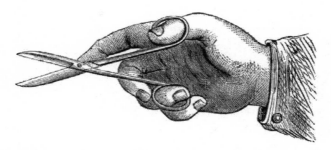

My parents owned and ran the drugstore in town for twelve years during the depression and war years. Six long, suspended rotating fans whirled above the shelves and counter of the drug store. The screen door, with its Nehi orange soda metal cross bar protecting the bowing mesh at its bottom, banged continually as the noontime patrons came to town to get their mail and goods. This door opening and closing with its squeaking spring suspension was music to a store owner's ears. The ice cream sundaes, malts, and cherry phosphates were a staple for the locals. The sweet smells of the spring produce wafted with the circulating air. The leather goods were well stocked in the apparel corner as the farmers sorted through the new selection of work gloves.

Drugstores in those days sold a collection of goods that ranged from shoes to bandages. These stores all had a soda fountain, candy, school supplies, over-the-counter remedies, personal hygiene products, fabric and watches. Conversation and advice was offered in the aisles. Managing the inventory during the dust bowl and watching families struggle to afford the basics was excruciatingly painful.

Farm families often did not have enough to eat or could not afford the coal to heat their homes. Extending credit was common. Livestock and grain prices sank to abysmal levels. Burning wood and cow chips was an economical source of fuel for the potbellied stoves.

My mother ran the store during the day while my dad farmed and managed the livestock. He came to the drugstore in the late afternoon to take over the counter while mother went home to get supper and tend to the children. We were to become a family of four children. The order of girl-boy-girl-boy was rather nice for balance of the sexes. I was the baby of the family. There was a sixteen-year difference between my oldest sister and me. The oldest two, Janie and Claude, were born during the depression years in 1932 and 1935. Our family income was supplemented by my parents' long hours and dedication to running the drugstore.

My next sister, Virginia, was born during WWII in 1943. The eight-year gap between babies was indicative of how extremely difficult the Dirty Thirties were for any farm family. By Virginia's birth, the hardships had eased. My mother had been a dancer and vocal performer in her youth. Bell's palsy struck her during her teenage years. Her beautiful, soprano voice was amazing considering the restrictions on the side of her face with the palsy. My father stopped at the drugstore to tell her that he had just come from the bank and paid Mr. Kirkpatrick the last payment on the mortgage on the home place. She was elated with joy. She did a dancer's leap and kicked her heels. The floor had just been mopped and the linoleum was like a sheet of ice. When she came down from her jump, she slipped and injured her tail bone. Its chronic pain always reminded her of the day the mortgage was burned.

My mother was also a registered nurse. Patrons and community members solicited her advice for every ailment, cold symptom, or cause of pain. Scrapes, bruises, and nagging injuries were discussed over the drugstore counter during the purchase of varied sundries. With no doctor for ten miles, Mother was the local medical advice center.

A great pandemic of polio was spreading across the country. This mysterious disease, which had struck down Franklin Roosevelt, was a worry for everyone. Children seemed especially vulnerable. It crippled 35,000 each year in the late 1940s and 50s. The March of Dimes was founded in 1938 with FDR's guidance to raise monies for treatment and research for a cure. Research for a vaccine was ongoing.

Every fall, the March of Dimes card was passed around the schools for the children to take home. One by one, dimes appeared across the line of slots until twenty partially visible dimes filled the card. These silver, ten-cent coins with FDR's embossed profile on them were emblematic of the cause. When the cards were filled, they were returned to the school teacher and pooled to mail to the authorities for accounting. Every child and family contributed. It did not seem a hardship on anyone, though the dimes were a sacrifice for many.

Theories and speculation for the spreading of the polio virus was rampant. Warnings to avoid large gatherings of people, washing hands, and being careful of getting colds and other common sniffles were issued.

In 1955, when a vaccine was discovered by Jonas Salk, everyone across the nation stood in lines for their multi-dose injections. Millions of school children received their vaccinations at school in the cafeteria or gymnasium assembly lines. Nurses with white uniforms and caps with credentialed pins on the front carefully drew up the serum, swabbed the upper left arm with pungent alcohol, and inserted the sharp needle into the brave awaiting child. The throbbing sensation of the vaccine bursting between the innocent muscle fibers was excruciatingly painful. Tears of anticipation and ensuing pain were commonly witnessed.

Was the polio virus getting into people's bodies through their tonsils? Doctors had started removing tonsils in the 1910s. Obviously, when these inflamed glands in the throat appeared, anxious surgeons quickly removed them. In the 1950s, two million tonsillectomies were being performed annually in the United States. Getting one's tonsils and adenoids out became a common procedure for anyone who dared to have a sore throat or two.

"They just went to the hospital to have their tonsils removed," or, "No big deal, it is a simple procedure." This was common talk, even around our small town of Bogue. If you consider masking down with ether, placing an endotracheal tube down the throat, and general anesthesia simple, then yes, it was an easy task for a surgeon. The surgical removal of these unwanted glands in the back of the throat usually included the removal of the adenoids. Who even knew what adenoids were, but they got whacked out as a matter of convenience, too, since the surgery was in the same general area.

As little boys, comparing anatomy was not considered important. Circumcision at birth was not even on the radar for discussion. At the age of seven, a child of the 50s had zippo for rights; consent forms were forty years away. When a kid was told he was going to have his tonsils removed, he just got in line like a lamb heading for slaughter. So, as you can imagine, waking up from anesthesia and being helped to the bathroom, I was shocked to drop my gown to find there was a bandage on my penis. I may have been naive but I was pretty sure that was *not* where the adenoids were located. Was this a surgeon's slip of the scalpel, or was it my first experience with non-disclosure of all the facts? I don't know if this incident ever made the front-page news, but to document my pain at least gives some closure to this unrequested snip job. All young boys getting their tonsils removed, this I advise; ask a few general questions on the procedure to be performed in advance to minimize surprises.

Nothing was ever mentioned by my parents. The ice cubes and snow cones following the tonsillectomy certainly were not palliative to my bandaged privates below. Not being able to get any sympathy from siblings or classmates was a bummer, too. In all the decades since, I have never seen this elective procedure mentioned on any surgery form or requested in any medical history questionnaire. No lines were ever formed under a sign saying, "circumcision at this door." No specials or discounts for multiple surgery options were ever advertised. Recovery was complete, and just being able to tell of this appendage alteration gives this farmer boy solace.

The polio epidemic, Asiatic influenza, and the proliferation of tonsillectomies all kept worried parents consulting the registered nurse behind the drugstore soda fountain. Hopefully, she was not recommending circumcision to all these families.

80CB

THREE OLD BAGS

The three cows standing in the milking parlor could not have been more different to me as a farmer boy. Old bags may sound inappropriate, but since that was another name for the cow udder, it sounded better than three old udders. I had personalized names for these three bossies. I called them Old Swissy, Black Baldy, and Red Bomber.

Old Swissy was a hand-me-down from my Uncle Ivan's milking herd. I had no idea what my dad could have bought or traded for this big momma. Why would Uncle Ivan have ever parted with such a good cow? Purebred dairies were the pride of dairyman. The black and white Holstein was the stereotypical dairy cow that Americans were most familiar with. The brown Swiss was native to Switzerland. They had the largest bone structure of all the dairy breeds. I loved Old Swissy. She was kind and obedient. She never kicked and was the easiest milker. Most importantly, she came into the barn without my having to chase her.

Old Swissy had the biggest set of faucets that I had ever seen. In human comparison, she was well endowed. She weighed nearly 1,200 pounds, but did not throw her weight around. Compared to a dancer, she would have been considered light on her feet. Her big, brown, placid eyes resembled those of a basset hound. Each year when she came into heat, my dad loaded her in the back of the truck and took her back to my uncle's Swiss bull for mating. She always complied and, year after year, blessed us with a large bull calf. Though getting a calf every twelve months and freshening was the ultimate goal, getting a heifer calf was more desired if looking for a future dairy cow for the herd.

Swissy's almost white bull calves were easily taught to drink from a bucket. I first inserted my fingers into their mouths so that they could suck on them just like nursing from their mother. Then when I gently pushed their heads down into a bucket to reach the milk at the bottom, they recognized the taste. The calf knew this was not momma and initially fought this new approach of receiving the white liquid nourishment. Blowing bubbles and an occasional slurp let them know that this was still good milk, just not from momma's teat. Over the course of a few days, each newborn could be taught to drink the milk without the simulation of my four fingers. They still loved to suck something. Some confused young calves would try sucking on another's ear. This was not encouraged. I offered my fingers. Though I had never heard of a pacifier for babies, fingers were the ultimate calf pacifier. As the calves grew, this magic finger pacifier seemed to always be soothing. Within a few weeks the calves were introduced to a molasses and oat-based grain mixture that resembled granola. It had a sweet aroma and flavor and was readily accepted by all young calves.

In time, as the calves became steers, they were placed into the feedlot with the beef calves. The Swiss calves were always bigger and their off-white, big-boned frames were easily distinguished in the pen of one-hundred steers. They never lost their pacifier love. Even as they topped 1,000 pounds, on their way to 1,500 pounds, I could call them over to the feed bunk and offer them my hand and they would suck my soiled, chore-callused fingers like they were candy. Petting them on the face with the other hand, they rubbed their faces and necks on my thread-bare, chore blue jeans. We were buddies again and reminisced about their bucket calf life.

When friends visited after school, they were introduced to the milk cows. What I considered a way of life, they thought was gross. They found the flies, smells, and manure repulsive, but calling a big steer over and seeing it carefully suck my fingers was out of this world.

Black Baldy was a barrel-chested cow we had raised from a calf. Her mother had been a kind, gentle, coal-black cow who had been mated to a beef Hereford, white faced, horned bull. Her mother died when she ate some fresh green fall sorghum and bloated. My dad had tried to stick a knife in her rumen to let off the methane gas, but it was too late. Black Baldy was the opposite of her barn mate Swissy. With her black body, white face, and patch of black over her right eye, she was a graceless klutz. Her faucets were small and they did not make for easy milking. She switched her tail continually and annoyed the milker with slaps across the face and neck. She would barge into the barn like she hadn't eaten in weeks. She quickly poked her greedy head through the other cows' stanchions and grab a bite of their grain before they could get to it. Cleverly, she ran to her stanchion like it was her right to eat others' rations, too. Black Baldy was an easy keeper. She "ate like a cow" and it all went to her hips. She kept all of this for her own maintenance and did not produce much milk. It could have been said that she was dumber than a box of rocks, but that would have been an insult to the rocks.

Red Bomber was the third cow in this colorful collection. In today's terms, this was a very diverse group. Bomber was one mean kicking machine. She was flighty and unpredictable. Her eyes darted back and forth and she acted like she never trusted anyone. She always required a set of kickers, an apparatus placed over the heels of the cow to reduce their ability to nail the milker with a swift unexpected blow with the back foot. I milked her last in hopes that my dad would finish his chores first and come help me finish.

Bomber always had a devious look on her face. She was a well-proportioned cow. She carried her weight well and her faucets were a bright pinkish red. As ornery as she was, she was an easy milker. She pulled back nervously when I tried to unlatch her wooden flap brace to release the stanchion. If she ever caught my hand, I got miffed and shouted out to let her know it. I retaliated by tossing a frightened cat upon her back. The claws and the yowling cat in retreat seemed to make things even.

We had a milking machine when my brother and sister were in charge of the chores. In my time, we were back to milking by hand. My dad could sit on the one-legged stool—it resembled a tee with a flat board nailed to a central square, foot-long pedestal which touched the floor—place the bucket between his legs, head in the flank of the cow, and milk a full pail in less than five minutes. He never seemed as interested in squirting the cats in their mouths as I did. Most of the cats would have wet faces after I became the primary milker, and the cats loved me.

When hand milking, the first few streams that hit the bottom of the stainless-steel pail reverberated with a sound similar to a high-pitched bullet. First one stream sounded with a quick second from another teat. The rhythm was not unlike a pendulum from a grandfather's clock. With every stream that hit the pail, a splashing sound grew more prominent as it slowly created a pool of milk in the pail. The forceful jets of white manna caused a bubbling action as it penetrated the milk surface of the pail. It was not unlike a foam on the surface of a head of beer. A good and easy milker could make the foam as thick as an inch.

Every cow's udder had a set of four teats that were unique in their size, shape, and positioning. The four quarters never varied, but the faucets could be quite different. The two front teats were often slightly larger. The resistance to the manual squeezing was distinct from cow to cow. Some were known as easy milkers and the stream of milk and the amount of milk was large as the hand kneaded around the doughy teat. The hard milkers had less capacity for volume in the teat cistern and the opening caused more resistance for the hand squeeze.

The easy milker allowed two hands to squeeze, alternating at a stroke of one per second—squeeze, release, squeeze, release, squeeze, release. With each squeeze, the pearly liquid propelled into the pail. When the hand released, the milk refilled the ventral hanging portal. The udder was an amazing labyrinth of sponge-like alveoli that, with gravity, allowed the milk to ooze ventrally as the pressure pushed the droplets downward. The vacuum caused by each stream of milk ejected quickly caused the teat to fill, ready for the next alternating hand squeeze.

It was most comfortable to sit on a one-legged stool with my legs apart, thus creating a tripod. Balancing on the stool became second nature and allowed for reaching beneath the cow to grab the faucets. First the front two teats and then the back two were milked. Sometimes, the diagonal pair were easier to put pressure and the squeeze-pulling motion gave a change of pace for young hands.

I was taught that anyone could learn to milk with time and patience. It was like riding a bike. Once you had the knack, it was never forgotten. The wrists and forearms became very strong. There was no manual exercise that built muscle in a kid's hands quite like milking cows. No one could out arm wrestle me, except perhaps another farm boy with the same chores and bigger hands.

I would put the grain on the manger floor, making sure the wooden two-by-four stanchions were open. Each cow got a proportional amount of grain, depending on her body size and how much milk she was making. After calving, or freshening as it is also called, the first few months were higher production times for milk volume.

At sixty days after freshening, the cow was rebred, either to a bull or by artificial insemination. The gradual reduction in the daily amount of milk produced seemed to coincide with the time when the rebreeding occurred. From then, it took nine months before a new calf was born. Nearing the time when the cow delivered her next calf, the milk production dropped considerably. The milking was reduced to once daily for a few days, and eventually ceased completely, thus drying her up. This "drying off" of the cow's production was time for her to catch up on her health and commit all her energy to the production of the new calf she carried inside. It gave the udder and mammary system a time of no production, thus restoring its health.

Since we only milked the three cows, I fed the cows with a one-pound Hills Brothers coffee can, measuring three, four, or five pounds per cow twice daily. When opening the barn door, there was a mad rush for each cow to get to her favorite stanchion. The grain was the enticing draw. First Baldy came with her mad rush. Old Swissy followed with her methodical, careful approach to the barn and she quietly slipped into her stanchion. Finally, I would have to go out into the corral and chase Bomber toward the open barn door. Tuffy, the cow dog and my constant companion, was always there to help. Bomber was leery of his nips. Tuffy would herd her. With a few disgusted snorts, she would run off in a mad rush for the open barn door and safety. While their heads pushed through the stanchions and the cows were head-down, eating the grain, I slid between them and flipped down the wooden supports, locking their necks between the hinged, wooden sides of the stanchion.

Having a pail of milk kicked over or a clumsy cow moving her back leg at the wrong time was a casualty if the milkman wasn't alert and careful. I never cried over spilt milk, but the cow sure heard a few blue words of reprimand.

A cow's tail could be a lethal weapon. Getting swatted a few times while sitting on the stool could set off the ire of a farmer boy who was trying to hurry the milking along. I would grab the bush of the tail, wrap a piece of baling twine around it, pulling the tail along the cow's side and tie the other end around her neck or to the front of the stanchion. This kept me from getting smacked. Even though swinging her tail was a reflex motion, not unlike a dog wagging its tail, this need to swing the tail was increased during fly season. For those times of year, a misting fly repellent spray was used from a hand-sprayer on the cow before milking.

One of the hazards of sitting on the milk stool came when leaning forward. It helped the balance to push your head nicely into the cow's flank. The hazard came when a hungry, straying louse made its way from the cow's hide onto my hair. It was never in doubt when the crawling sensation sped across the top of my towheaded scalp. An essential shampooing before school alleviated the problem.

When visitors or cousins came to the farm, they followed me around as I did my chores. Everyone wanted to help milk the cows. After a few unproductive strokes, they would give up. It was like trying to pick a guitar; it always looked so much easier than it actually was. To this day, I can milk a cow with no refresher course even though it has been over a half century. Though this skill is no longer very marketable, or even visible to your friends, it is a hidden talent I am proud to possess.

Turning the cows out of the stanchions took a knack as keen as catching them in the first place. Flipping the wooden brace stopper up could be done right down the line—one, two, three, four. The only problem was if I wasn't quite quick enough to get my fingers under the flap before the cow pulled her head and neck back. This either put too much pressure on the wooden flap, or it would catch my fingers, causing a sharp pain and few "dad-burn-its!"

One day as I went to get the cows, I noticed Black Baldy waddling and slowly making her way up the path. Her sides were puffed and bloated tight as a drum. She was having a hard time breathing as the extended rumen was pushing forward onto her diaphragm. She was not able to expand her lungs and her cyanotic blue tongue hung out of her opened mouth. A few steps after passing through the gate near the chicken house, she collapsed onto her right side. The moaning, bellowing sound was exactly like that of her mother's before she died. I threw down the egg bucket and raced to the house. I fetched one of my mother's long butcher knives and sprinted back to the downed and paddling cow. Without hesitation, I lifted the knife over my head, grasping it in both hands. With one mighty downward stoke, I jabbed the sharp knife into Baldy's side just in front of her pelvic bone. The instantaneous blast of pungent methane gas came exploding around the puncture with the knife still in place. The gas was accented with the fresh, fall, green alfalfa that Baldy had overeaten. This gluttonous old bag had nearly eaten her last meal. The deflation of a bloated cow happens much like a punctured balloon. Baldy groaned a few agonizing sounds and puffed a breath of air. Slowly, she took another slightly longer breath, and finally some labored, but normal deep breaths followed. She had been within seconds of ending up in the bone pile. I helped her get up and she staggered to the barn corral. Dad was just getting home with the tractor and the chisel plow. He opened the gate and helped me get Baldy into the barn.

"Nice job, son. She must have really been out of it for you to be able to trocar her," he said matter-of-factly. His calmness reflected the life of an animal caretaker who has had to deal with every emergency with a cool head.

"Yeah, if I hadn't seen you stick her mother, I wouldn't have known what to do," I replied, acting like this was an everyday occurrence. "Do we leave that knife in her? Or when do we pull it out?" I asked.

Dad smiled and looked a little puzzled. "To tell you the truth son, she may be the first one that I have ever seen live and not croak. Getting that pressure released in time on a severe bloat has to be timely." We both laughed and grinned at our predicament. "I think we just pull it out in a few more minutes and see what happens," Dad said.

"Works for me, but why don't you pull it out?" I answered.

With one motion, Dad quickly yanked the protruding knife from the cow's belly. Baldy just stood there looking rather dumbfounded like it did not hurt one bit. "I am proud of you and great job," Dad said again. Those words from a father were golden. We did not say the word love often, but this was as close as it got between a father and son

I did not feed Baldy that night, and she did not give over an inch of milk. Dad went on to do the pig and feedlot chores and I milked the others as usual. The next morning as I opened the door to let the cows into their stanchions, the first one barging through the door was that goofy Black Baldy. She did not miss a meal, but was quarantined from any fresh green alfalfa or sorghum until after it had frosted and the rich state for fermentation had passed.

It was just another day in a twelve-year old farmer boy's life. Baldy lived to be an old cow and her habits continued until the day she died.

&⬥&

BIRDS OF ALL FEATHERS

Shooting sparrows with a flashlight and a BB gun was like forking fish in a barrel. They were blinded by the light and left defenseless. To get fifteen to twenty sparrows in one night was not uncommon. This hunt was necessary on the farm as these birds were pests and ate the grain in the fields, the barn granaries, and the feed bunks with the cattle. A sparrow was a sparrow, regardless how many different kinds there were. Climbing up on the rafters in the big red barn and steadying a BB gun at night with only a flashlight for guidance was tricky. This was a job better performed solo. Whenever additional town friends, cousins, or nephews accompanied me on this mission, pandemonium occurred. The least of the dangers was slipping and falling the twenty-odd feet to the hard dirt and concrete floor of the barn below.

Starlings were another story altogether. They were smaller than a crow, ate more grain, and scavenged worse than sparrows. Since starlings were black, they were harder to spot with a light. They were also more skittish. After a shot or two, they became alarmed and flew even though it was pitch dark. They could be heard flapping their wings and occasionally hitting a rafter support. They stirred up the chop and grain dust from the cross-support beams and would come to rest on the planks leading across the walkways.

As I got braver, I could balance and walk on the six-inch-wide rafters in the dark to get to the middle beam. This gave me a great "cat bird's seat" view of more vulnerable grain bandits above. Having an airborne, wing flapping starling hit me from the back or in the face was creepy, but just one of the hazards of my efforts to reduce the bird population. I received my Daisy pump BB gun for Christmas. Every kid had at least one gun, though none was as good a shot as I. The flashlight was held along the left side of the barrel and the gun was aimed so that the sight at the tip could barely be seen and focused on the target. After gently pulling the feather-light trigger, the sparrow came cascading down in a freefall to the barn floor. A mad scramble ensued below as the awaiting cats responded to the deadening flop. Mealtime for the many scavenger cats was never so easy. Their growls over trying to protect their easy prey soon dissipated as the many falling birds gave each cat a delicious meal.

Daytime ventures led to the barns and many elm trees on the farmstead. I could spot a bird's nest in the bow of any tree. I could tell the difference between sparrow and starling nests from the nests other birds. Climbing trees to pull down nests was another method of controlling the bird population.

I would never, however, disturb a nest of robins or song birds. The most elaborate swinging basket nest of the Baltimore oriole was of exquisite construction. King birds would test a tow-headed kid making cat-like progress along the branches to a nest. These king birds defended their turf with a fury and would dive bomb me with aggressive swoops toward my head.

The farm cats knew the drill. When a ladder was propped against a tree, they knew there was a possibility of falling baby birds. I preferred to get the nests down before the babies hatched. Dropping a nest to the ground with the white speckled eggs seemed much less ruthless than sending one down with babies awaiting the return of their mothers with their beaks open and necks stretched skyward.

This method of birth control was an ongoing battle. A sparrow could build a new nest in a day. My marauding ventures on sparrows would at least force them to another tree.

Barn swallows were off limits altogether for this farmer boy. Even though they would dive bomb the farm cats, I thought they were so graceful and beautiful with their purple and black-ish sheen. Their chirp and v-shaped tail feathers made their flight with bobbing and weaving a delight to watch. They al-ways seemed to come back each spring to the place they had left the previous fall. The swallows of Capistrano could not have been more loyal. Their artistic skill of building a nest out of small sticks and mud was incredible. I watched the progress of nest-building daily and it was not unlike watching a multi-story building taking shape. The fresh mud from the day's building would not be dried by the evening milking of the cows, but twelve hours later, in the morning, it was dry and the fresh, dark, moist mud a grayish color. How they knew when to add a twig or leaf stem was a mystery. They lined the perfectly shaped nest with the softest feathers, either from the chickens in the barnyard or from the ubiquitous sparrow feathers they spot-ted on the ground.

The male swallows stood watch over the nests. They sat on nearby utility or electric wires near the barn. The female laid four or five eggs. Though I was not privy to knowing, I believed they were much like a chicken and only laid one egg per day. These gorgeous little blue eggs were seen when I peeked at them while standing on a step stool. I never touched them and only looked upon them when the daddy swallow was off on a hunt. The nervous mother chattered and scolded me. I marveled at the symmetry and the architectural design of their creation and impatiently waited while she sat on those eggs. I never knew exactly how long it took for the eggs to hatch. The mother swallow's little head and beak rested motionless over the edge of the nest, and she never seemed to leave. In about two weeks, a noise came from the mud adobe. Within days, a constant de-livery system of food morsels was brought airmail by both the male and female swallows. The hatchlings squawked in antici-pation with each arrival. They, too, propped their beaks with their bright yellow lining over the sides of the mud home. Six-teen days after hatching, the babies took flight. Awkward at first, they often hit the side walls of the barn or adjacent concrete, stave silo. I rushed to their rescue and gently scooped them up and placed them on a branch in the peach tree alongside the barn. The farm cat brigade was ever-present, so these rescue missions were necessary to save these gorgeous new little swallows.

My tree climbing days came to an end with a harrowing experience. I was high up in an elm tree, out on a lateral branch near what seemed to be a raised nodule on the branch leading to the far away sparrow's nest. I slipped and fell some thirty feet to the hard ground below. My friend and neighbor, Allen Gosselin, was over that day playing. His tree climbing skills were inept, so he was on the ground, coaching my poaching venture. As I fell, he contemplated catching me, but wisely dodged my falling body as I hit the ground with a thud. I fell on my left side and didn't hear any crunching or cracking sounds on impact. I lay still on the cool, moist soil for a few moments before attempting to get to my feet. Allen consoled me and dusted off my jeans. I was woozy and wanted to lie down. Allen threatened that if I wouldn't play, he was going home.

"Go ahead," I said. "I'm going to go to the trailer house to lie down." It was dinnertime and our usual fried chicken, mashed potatoes and gravy with a side serving of vegetables and Jell-O salad waited, but I had no appetite and told my mother I was tired and just wanted to lie down.

It was a cool, cloudy day with a storm brewing in the west. An eerie wind gusted and then calmed, creating a constant rustling in the cottonwood trees. I curled up and closed my eyes. The world seemed to be spinning. I did not know if I was dreaming or if the flashes that were darting across my closed eyelids were shooting stars. Four hours later, my mother touched my shoulder.

"Jimmy, Jimmy, can you wake up?" Mother begged. "You've been sleeping all afternoon. Are you all right?"

With my cheeks distended with air, I gradually exhaled a steady, long sigh. "Yep, is dinner ready?" I blurrily replied, trying to focus on my surroundings.

"Why, yes, we ate four hours ago. It is almost time for chores and supper," she said, and coaxed me for a reason for my fogginess.

I was laying on the sofa in my brother's trailer where his wife Barbara had been watching me. A concussion was the probable reason for my lassitude, but I never fessed up to falling from that tree during my hunt. If I had, I am sure I would have received more medical attention.

After this close call falling from the tree, my nest marauding escapades ended. I moved on to trying to save every little creature, great and small. To think that a concussion could have transformed me into a James Audubon enthusiast would have been the furthest thing from my mind.

෨෬

James Kenyon

THE FARM HORSE

By the time of my childhood, the need for a horse to work the fields had been replaced by the gasoline engine. The green, two-cylinder Waterloo Boy started this revolution. The draft horse was relegated to Amish farmers and horse aficionados.

Any farm that had cattle, however, still had a horse to round-up or move the cattle from paddocks, barnyards, or pastures. My three siblings were much older than me, yet we all had experience with Tony, our family's horse.

Tony was a striking, black beauty gelding that came to my dad through a trade. Pinky King, a local wrangler, had roped this black yearling in the Colorado Mountains as a wild mustang on the open range. The rope burn on his back fetlock left a scar he carried the rest of his life. Pinky struggled to teach Tony about being a nice cutting and riding horse. My dad noticed him running in a pasture alongside the blacktop near Pinky's small farm. Dad inquired about him, and Pinky was happy to say that the black devil was for sale. Dad and Pinky agreed to trade an old saddle for the horse. Tony came home that day to live with us for the next thirty-one years of his life.

Dad loved a good horse. When he climbed up in the saddle in his bibbed overalls, he hardly looked like Roy Rogers, but with his straw hat pulled low and work boots locked into the stirrups, he transformed into a cowboy.

Tony was a natural cattle horse. His ability to separate out a cow in the herd was instinctive. When he worked his way into a grouping of cows, he was always calm and could push to the center of the herd with ease. Dad only gave him a slight rein and the combat was on. Tony would get the eye of the cow and carefully juke and bob his head as the cow nervously tried to move away into the herd. Slowly, Tony was reined and nudged by Dad's knees as they worked back and forth in this game of showmanship. The showdown was somewhat like a base runner caught in a rundown. The ball player with the ball faked and bobbed his body as they moved forward. Older cows knew from experience that after about three or four short dashes to the left and right, their goose was cooked. The cow would give up and head toward the gate or the pen opening.

I always took these cutting sessions for granted. Neither my dad nor Tony had professional training. The team had not watched a video on how to cut out a steer. The natural instinct, the symmetry, and the ability to use the legs and reins to maneuver the horse into position was innate. When Tony was home in our barnyard, he shared the paddock with the milk cows. He sometimes was caught separating out one of the cows on his own as if it was a game. A milk cow was usually not as nimble as a beef cow. With their milk factory swinging like a pendulum between their back legs, they were no challenge for Tony's piercing eye. Two jukes of his head and a sideways move, and the poor old Holstein was cornered.

The daytime pasture for the milk cows was about one-half mile down the sandy, gravel road to a long narrow lane. There was never any traffic or vehicles passing by; when the barnyard gate was opened, the small troop of cows headed out each morning after milking for greener pastures. One of us kids rode Tony bareback and followed the cows out to head them west. A cow could have just eaten the best meal of ground corn, silage, and fresh green hay, but given a weed or anything green along the way, she stopped to munch like she hadn't eaten in weeks. Since the cow had no teeth on her upper front mouth pad, she had to bite hard and yank her head up or sideways to tear off an unsuspecting sunflower or lush, succulent pigweed. Usually, the whole plant was uprooted and old bossy was content to walk down the road with the plant dangling until she had maneuvered the whole weed into her mouth.

There were always leaders and laggards. My favorite cows were those who hurried along the half mile, then down the long, narrow lane and into the pasture ahead. With the morning sunlight poking through the distant, tall elms surrounding our farmstead, this caravan went down the sunflower-lined lane. It was the job of the farm kid to close the gate after the cows and dash back home upon Tony like a black bolt of lightning. Holding on was the goal. With the left hand wrapped tightly in a handful of mane and the sweaty, gripped reins in the other, we were off to the races. There was no slowing or stopping that horse when he was headed home. Whether he intended it or not, when he turned the corner at the end of the lane, he came within a millimeter of the corner fence post with his body. Tony ran like he was at the Indy 500, banking and then hitting the corner at maximum speed. Any rider with sense at all knew to anticipate this antic and was fluid in throwing his inside leg up over the horse's back to keep from getting scraped-off by the corner post. My sister Janie would be infuriated with Tony as, more than once, she ended up in a heap on the ground. She would walk home kicking pebbles and mumbling under her breath while Tony was already back in the barnyard paddock eating fresh Timothy hay. Either a farm hand or my dad would have taken off his bridle and patted him on the underserving rump as he sauntered off to the feed manger, a look of nonchalance on his face.

A few minutes later, Janie arrived with her dusty jeans and scraped elbow, swearing at that darned horse. She vowed that he would never dump her again. It was amazing how quickly Tony was forgiven as the option of walking a mile out and a mile back came around the next day. Inevitably, my sister would slip Tony's bridle on, lead him to the fence, climb on the lower rail, and jump on his back for a repeat performance and adventure. Janie was tough and smart, so repeated scrape-offs were rare.

By the time I was old enough to be the one with the chore of taking the cows to and from to the pasture, Tony was older and maybe had mellowed. He never managed to peel me off in this game. Flying bareback, hunkered down for the race was still the fastest way home. I liked to experience the speed and the challenge of each morning's escapade while holding on bareback to this wonderful steed.

On school days, my dad took the cows out across the road to graze the green wheat or milo stubble. The cows only went to the pasture throughout the summer months. During school months, Tony was only needed in the evenings to get the cows. He looked forward to this duty as much as he loved to run home or try his trick at corner-post scraping. The old horse accepted the bit readily in his mouth and the bridle was easily slipped over his head. I was just tall enough to grab some mane with one hand, pump my legs a few times and throw myself up with one leg to mount him. This maneuver was like the western movies and the Indians with their buckskin clothes and moccasins easily mounting a moving pony.

Riding bareback brought a boy and horse into one, moving, compact unit. Feeling the muscles, the power, and every motion between the legs of the rider made these pounding, dashing hoofbeats reverberate through my body. It was so much easier than having to carry a heavy, cumbersome saddle off its pedestal perch, dust it off, making sure the stirrups were free, and hoisting it over the back of a sometimes moving target. Before I was tall enough to lift and place this inverted, boat-shaped apparatus with dangling stirrups and girth onto the horse's back, I had to stand on an inverted, five-gallon bucket. Doing this by myself required tying Tony to the board fence, getting a blanket and saddle, climbing up on the bucket, and flailing the saddle up over Tony's back. If lucky, I made it on the first attempt, the horse wouldn't move, and the bucket didn't topple. Then I had to reach under the horse to pull the girth up to start cinching it into place with the leather girth strap. Tony had a habit of inhaling and holding his big, distended chest out full so that it was arduous to get the cinch tight enough. My dad would give Tony a quick knee to his belly, causing him to exhale so that the cinch could be tightened at the same time. It was impossible for me to bring my knee high enough to have the same effect. A loose saddle made the ride very precarious. When possible, I always preferred to ride without a saddle.

My cousin, Janet Petersen, visited with her grandparents every summer from California. They would stay in their camper in our backyard for weeks. She was four years older, but she was the ultimate tomboy. There was not a tree she couldn't climb or an animal chore that wasn't fun in Janet's eyes.

One afternoon Janet and I thought it would be a great day to ride Tony. I had ridden tandem bareback before, but it was not the easiest to balance. Holding on for the person in the back was difficult. With only one hand clinching the mane, this clumsy positioning could easily lead to a pileup. So out came the heavy, cumbersome saddle. I was eight at the time and with Janet's help I managed to hoist the leather load on to Tony's back. I did my best to cinch the saddle as I had watched my father do many times. The knee to the horse's belly, the exhale, and the quick tightening of the cinch seemed to secure the saddle.

Janet was a big girl and very strong. I helped her get up on Tony. The horse knew these two greenhorns were up to something unusual for him. After a few times around the horse paddock, I put my left foot in the stirrup and scurried up on Tony behind Janet who was filling the saddle. Sitting behind a saddle in a copilot position, a person has only two things to hold on to—the pummel or the waist of the person in front. I had already opened the paddock gate, so out into the yard and down the road this tandem duo went for a ride.

I never cleared such activities with my parents. Farm boys had the latitude to play and explore outside on their own. It was on this adventure that I realized that the saddle was sliding and not as secure as I would have liked. At first, it only shifted a bit to the left and then the right as we cousins set off in a gallop.

Tony had always had a fear about anything around his back feet. Since his capture by the rope around his back foot, any wire or dangling leather strap, or even a tangled weed around his foot, would set this docile steed into a panic. We headed down the cow lane, opened the pasture gate, and set off across the buffalo grass pasture to Arbuthnot's Grove. The June flower growth of wild Black-eyed Susans, pink roses, and a sprinkling of yucca plants made a perfectly beautiful setting for these two young cowhands. The meadowlarks fluttered from fencepost to fencepost in front of us as they accompanied us down the lane into the pasture. A lone jackrabbit bounced and serpentined across the path in front of the two cowhands.

The separating contrails of two air force jets fluttered high above the distant tree line. Sweating in the warm, June, midday sun, the greenhorns set off across the prairie. A few wispy clouds strung lazily in the ocean-blue sky.

Insects are attracted to a horse. With very thin skin, a horse is sensitive to stinging and buzzing bugs. A large horse fly biting can drive the horse into a frenzy. Flies bite at their pasterns and their exposed undersides. Sweat bees and black bumble bees can also pester horses.

The rider is also bothered by these varmints, but can usually ward them off by swatting or shooing them away. I had put some fly repellent on a rag and rubbed it onto Tony's legs before we put the bridle on him. Sweating and evaporation could cause even the best efforts to prevent pests to fail. It may have been a large horse fly, or even a dangling strap off the saddle horn, but something spooked Tony and we set off on one of the fastest gallops I had ever experienced. Had I been bareback, there would have been no problem. But with inexperienced Janet at the helm, a loose saddle, and me holding on for dear life, we set off across the hard, bare pasture at break-neck speed.

"Tony! Stop! Stop!" I yelled at the top of my lungs. My pleading was to no avail. No matter how hard Janet pulled back on the reins, which worked the bit in Tony's mouth, he refused to slow.

When the horse had taken me for such jaunts before, I had a trick that usually stopped him in his tracks. Though it was dangerous, I would throw the reins down in front of his front feet and the threat of stepping on them caused him to slow down and stop. I could then shimmy down and grab the reins and he was mine to control again. Tony seemed to honor this maneuver and gave this little cowboy credit for outwitting the old steed.

But on this day, this option did not seem a great choice. Should he stumble by stepping on the thrown reins, he would toss both of us into a catapulting heap. I frantically yelled to Janet. There was no other choice but to try. As we were approaching the woods, the reins were thrown. Tony turned sharply to the left; the saddle and the two cowhands went flying off. The dust flew as our bodies and the hard ground met abruptly.

"Are you okay?" I anxiously blurted to Janet.

She moaned an affirmative and asked, "How about you?"

"There's no blood, but my arm may be broken," I said, as I surveyed my misaligned, right forearm.

We untangled our legs and crawled out from under the saddle there on the brick-hard ground. I stood up and gazed about to take in the surroundings. Cacti were all around us, but somehow in the fall we had missed landing in them. Tony stopped only a few steps away and came back and nuzzled me. The sweat and froth on his neck were evidence that the long run had been exhilarating. Forgiving him was easy, and I decided it was probably a horse fly that had set him off.

"Do you think you can help me throw the saddle up on his back and we'll fix the stirrups up over the saddle horn so they don't dangle?" I asked, and summoned Janet with my plan.

"We can try, but I think I can do it myself," Janet answered. She grunted as she managed to get the saddle blanket into place and a burst of energy allowed her to place the saddle squarely on Tony's back on the first try. Tony must have known that this was not a happy troop and he didn't move as the saddle came flopping on his back by this tinhorn.

I was not able to move my right arm as it trembled and started to show a blanching color change. "We can take our socks off and make a sling," Janet offered.

"Na, let's just get hoofing it. We have at least a mile to go to get home. I can tough it out, but why don't you lead Tony?" I winched with the pain and we slowly began the trek home. The clouds in the west were bellying down to the horizon. A huge harvest moon peeked up in the east. The meadowlarks still bobbed from each perch along the way. We dodged the cactus and yucca while meandering through the lane to finally reach home.

The trip to the doctor was uneventful. My mother had put an ice pack around my swollen wing. She tied a dish towel around my neck which cradled the throbbing arm. Dr. Kobler looked at the X-ray and told my mother and me that he would set the arm and apply a plaster of Paris cast. I didn't know what setting the arm entailed, but was soon to find out.

He should have given me a bullet to clamp down on, but no pain relief medication was offered. Grabbing my hand in his and holding the elbow in his other hand, he gave my arm three hard tugs and seemed satisfied that his manipulations had worked. The broken ends of the radius and ulna seemed to be back in alignment. The shock of such a yanking movement sent pain waves through my body. I was in enough pain that I couldn't fend off much, but felt determined that this darned doctor was not going to get another chance to set my arm. No tears for this cowboy, but to this day I am sensitive to the excruciating pain of a broken limb. I always give some medical pain relief for any animal before trying to set and get a bone back in place.

Three weeks of a heavy, full-arm white cast were ahead. The sweat and rubbing around the bicep was all part of the healing. The most comfortable position was to put my arm up over my head and off to chores I would go. There were eggs to be gathered, cows to feed, and the horse to curry and reminisce with about our accident. Tony seemed to understand, though I was sure I was giving him some slack for believing that he had anything to do with this hard, white club impairment around my limb. I would get some cow manure on the outside of the cast which I would attempt to wash off in the water tank. It came off, but there was a telltale greenish stain left behind. The cattle feed and dust of scooping the feed filled the air and settled around the top of the cast.

I wrote my sister in Texas a letter and proudly told her I was writing with my left hand. My scribbled words looked like a child's first attempts to write his name.

The cast came off in the doctor's office. The saw that reverberated down the side, the powdered smoke filling the air, and the separation of the two pieces revealed a stained and soiled cast padding wrap beneath the cast. A pungent aroma filled the air as it was unraveled. There was a milo seed and two wheat kernels that had accidentally entered from the top of the cast. A broken arm had not stopped me from doing routine farm chores. The seeds had started to sprout, and their hulls were moist and separating. Under the padding was the iodine-stained arm with only a slight bruise. The fracture had apparently healed. This lesson of quick mending stayed with me for all of my veterinary practice years. It only takes a few days or weeks of stationary confinement in a cast to get a good callus around a fracture site. Getting the cast off quickly prevents the massive amount of rehabilitation, the atrophy, and emaciation that can occur by leaving a cast on too long.

Telling a farm boy to be careful fell on deaf ears. Babying an arm was never in the equation. It was back to work and there were chores to do, but it was much like a toddler with a pacifier or sucking a thumb. When my parents weren't watching, the arm would go back over the top of my head just to rest it and get some comfort and reprieve of the downward pressure.

Janet returned to California for another year. The wheat harvest, baseball practice, and the 4-H County Fair were all still to come. It was not a bragging story to admit to the other kids that I had broken my arm falling off a horse. They never heard the true story, as falling off a horse with a girl was just not something to advertise.

Every morning and evening before the milk cows were let into the barn, Tony got his can of grain on a smooth concrete slab by the silo. He soon shared the slab with another filly, Babe. Babe, was a sorrel quarter horse, the daughter of Irish, who was Reverend Martin's stallion. Though Tony's cattle days ended with the coming of the new filly, he remained a prominent fixture in the limestone barn and paddock.

I knew our horse was aging when he started losing weight. No matter how much I fed him, his ribs started showing. His walked stiffened and his face became more elongated. His beautiful, dark eyes looked distant and his whinny and nicker at feeding time were much fainter.

One afternoon as I walked across the field coming home from school, I did not see Tony in the paddock. I changed clothes and ran to the barn to see where he was. There on the north side of the limestone cow barn, he was down and unable to rise. He tried several times to lift his head only to have it flop back down on the padded barn floor. He nickered and groaned as he tried again to greet me.

"Tony, my Tony! I am so sorry," I said as I rubbed his sweating face. "I knew you were fading, but how, oh how! I didn't know that I would find you like this."

I softly spoke to him. I laid down and patted his head and caressed his once powerful neck and sides. He was breathing more rapidly and tears ran down my flushed cheeks. I knew that his final day had come, and there was nothing my dad or I could do to stop it. I brought the old horse a bucket of water and lifted his neck so that he could take some long swallows of the cold liquid.

Dad was already doing the hog and cattle chores. He came into the barn to find us laying together there. I know that he had already seen Tony down, so I didn't need to choke out any words to him. I am sure he wouldn't have been able to say anything easily through his stoic facial reactions.

"Son, I found him this way earlier today. You know there is nothing we can do except help get some softer bedding under him," Dad muttered with a quiet breath.

"He knew how much we loved him. He has brought us all so much joy," he continued.

"I know Dad. It just seems that he has always been here for us," I choked.

"Son, you helped take care of him during your years. He loved you too," Dad said as he put his arm around me and I hugged his waist.

The next morning, Tony was dead. My dad took his body out into the pasture and dug a hole with the front-end loader. Though I was to love Babe and other horses in my future, this black mustang was the most incredible horse friend I ever had.

ಬಿ⊂ಞ

James Kenyon

GRANDSTANDING

Bounce, bounce, bounce—deep breath—bounce, bounce—deep breath—bounce—deep breath, exhale... Aim ... a perfect shot from the free throw line. The two-handed toss banked off the wooden backboard and dropped through the awaiting cylinder and net.

"And that would be another score for Wilt as the Jayhawks take the lead," Max Falkenstein would announce over WIBW radio. My make-believe games with my hero went on daily, before and after chores, until it was dark outside. The egg bucket sat by the cottonwood tree while the rubber Wilson basketball was dribbled and pounded through the hoop.

I mimicked Wilt's underhanded free-throw delivery. This was the only way an eight-year old farmer boy could reach the goal. Standing behind a line drawn in the dirt with a stick, I attempted the charity free throw.

"The ball is advanced up the court by John Parker. Into the left corner to Bob Billings and a quick bounce pass into Chamberlain. He fakes left. There are three Sooners hanging all over him. Wilt dribbles out and shoots a right-handed hook. He scores! He scores!" I excitedly announced while out of breath with exhilaration. "The final seconds tick off the clock and that's the game, folks. The Jayhawks stay perfect at home this year, pulling away the last few minutes against the Sooners. We'll be right back after this word from Ralston Purina, the checkerboard people."

"Jimmy, it's time for supper. Be sure to bring in the eggs," my mother called from the back porch.

Dad and I built the square backboard during the winter. The new basketball had come from Santa and was under the artificial, pink metal Christmas tree. We bolted the official orange rim to the freshly painted backboard. The long pole was attached and slowly lifted with the tractor hoist, then dropped into the deep hole dug with the posthole diggers. A quick concrete mix was poured into the hole securing the basketball post.

My brother invited Mom, Dad, and me to a game in Lawrence to see the fabulous sophomore, Wilt Chamberlin. He effortlessly scored forty points that night. The seven-footer with his knee-high socks seemed a giant to me. From that night forward, I listened to every game on the radio. The make-believe games dribbling, passing, and shooting on the dirt court around the high goal honed the imagination.

Mr. Clayton was the new school principal. He was six-foot-four and towered over the elementary children. He had played basketball at Sterling College. For physical education, the gray folding chairs were arranged on the gymnasium floor. All the boys and girls lined up and the basketball dribbling drills began. Bouncing balls echoed as the methodical training proceeded with everyone learning to dribble. Around the chair on the left with the left hand, then switching to the right hand to go around the chair on the right, and so forth, until the neophyte basketball player reached the other end of the gym and handed off to another player going the other way.

Balls clanged off the chair legs and went bounding away from the rescuing third grader. Feet got tangled and an off-the-foot bounce would send the round ball squirting down the court. Day after day the drills consumed the half-hour PE time slot. Farm kids, town kids, tall kids, and small kids, we all learned to bounce pass, underhand shuffle pass, and hook pass.

The third-grade boys and the fourth-grade boys scrimmaged during noon recess. Sweaty students frequented the water fountain before and during class periods. The round ball became synonymous to the indoor winter recesses.

By the fifth grade, basketball games with other small towns were scheduled. Playing in other gyms, each having their own characteristics, was an adventure for these elementary aged boys. Some were some small gyms where the out-of-bounds line was the wall. At the other end of the spectrum were gyms with a small stage for the cheerleaders and spectators. Night games were special as the school bus transported us out of town. We carried duffle bags full of our gear. The pep squad and cheerleaders' bus followed us, their heroes, with enthusiasm.

Decked out in deep red jerseys and shorts, these round-ballers emerged from the locker room. The satin, crimson warmup jackets with Bogue Cardinals on the back were distinctive for the team. My number was 22. It was a magic number for me that I chose for every sports jersey thereafter.

Our last games of the season took place at the eight-team tournament in Zurick where the court doubled as the school cafeteria. The floor had hard vinyl tiles, two-feet squares of irregular patterns. The ball bounced differently than on a hardwood court. Getting used to this feel and was essential to competing against some of the best teams.

The tournament was a midgets' tourney. That name was deceiving as there were no particularly short, undersized players or teams. Midgets, in this case, was a set of criteria to even out the tall boys and the smaller ones. It was based on player weight. No one over ninety-five pounds was allowed to play. An official weigh-in took place before the first game. If a player was one ounce over the ninety-five pounds, he was off the playing roster. Ronnie Stephens had porked up and was not qualified. This may have been much like modern day wrestlers trying to make weight. Our five starters were one eighth grader, one seventh grader, and three sixth graders—Johnny Adams, Steve Davignon, cousin Alan, cousin Layton, and me. Mr. Clayton had us run drills and passing for layups before the first tournament game. We slowly adjusted to the hard bounces and managed to pull away in the second half.

While we were showering and dressing after the game, Coach Clayton asked everyone to take a seat on the gray benches in the locker room. We sat at attention, awaiting this unusual post-game team meeting. With a long, serious face, he started his speech. "I am okay with the outcome of our game tonight. But, I want to address to all of you and to two of you, in particular, about grandstanding," he droned. "Grandstanding is the worst thing you can ever do in any sport," he continued. We sat pensively, waiting for the next shoe to drop. Only our eyes moved as we looked around to see who the two players may have been.

"Jimmy, you and Steve are good players, but, your actions tonight are not acceptable. Grandstanding to draw attention to yourself is demeaning. When you make exaggerated leaps to intercept a pass out of your range, it is obvious that you are playing to the crowd," he said, seriously lecturing.

This tow-headed farmer boy was crushed. I did not realize that I had been acting in such a showoff manner. With my head tucked and a somber face, I rode the eighteen miles home without saying a word to anyone. To be scolded in private was one thing, but in front of the whole team was devastating.

The next night, the second tournament game was also a victory, but there was no more drawing attention by any of the ten boys who played for the Cardinals. No one was praised for their performance. The locker room was quiet. There was concern and trouble ahead. The Woodston Coyotes played in the other semifinal game of the tournament. They were not only good, they blew away their opponent, Plainville Sacred Heart. We had never witnessed a team that could fast break on every play. Their passing was phenomenal. They were tall and lanky, and it looked like they might blow us off the court the next night.

On the way home that night Coach Clayton stood in front of the bus and faced the parallel rows of seats filled with his team. He solemnly announced, "Our game tomorrow night for the championship is set for seven o'clock. I want all of you to get a good night's sleep tonight. Tomorrow being Saturday, there is to be no hard work and maybe even a nap in the afternoon. I want you all at the gym at five o'clock as we are going to practice a new defense. That is all. You'll see what I have planned when you arrive," he said, finally finishing his instructions.

Doing the farm chores, milking, and helping Dad with the cattle—to me, none of this was work. Tuffy and I pulled the red wagon and delivered the eggs to my loyal customers, as usual. Naps were out of the question, but I did not play any make-believe games on my dirt court.

I worried and fretted all day, wondering just what new defense the coach was going to employ. I could remember the high-flying Woodston team strutting and so confident on the court. Was I going to be starting? Was the grandstanding speech going to come again? There was no rest as I quickly finished gathering the evening eggs. I ate an early supper before arriving for the five o'clock practice.

"Tonight we have about forty-five minutes to learn what is called a full court press. I believe we can surprise them with a new wrinkle that will stop them and slow down their run and gun fast break," Coach Clayton said, confidently lecturing the boys sitting on the bleachers. Mr. Clayton, with his massive size and straight face, always had our full attention. Tonight, he seemed even more serious.

We were all in our street clothes.

"Okay, I want the five who are not starters to take out the ball. Jimmy and Layton, you stand here in the forecourt. Steve and Alan, you are behind them here, and Johnny, you will be back under the basket. This is a 2-2-1 press defense. You all will have opportunities to double team, steal the ball, and intercept errant and hurried passes," Coach said as he demonstrated. "So no one will be on the guy throwing in the ball. Try to intercept the incoming pass but don't let the ball come to the center court. Push the offense to the corner and double team. When possible, keep your spacing and always think of yourself covering your own quarter of the forecourt. Think **2-2-1**," Coach instructed as he flipped the ball to Mike Bellerive to in-ball.

The instructions and drills were hurried. Mr. Pricer, the assistant, pointed out the time to force the turnover and from where to watch for the futile hurried pass. The time flew by as we shuffled and went through the plays in the dimmed light of the gym.

We were all smiles as we stepped off the bus at the Zurick school. The parking lot was full, and the noise coming from the gym for the consolation game could be heard outside in the crisp March air.

During the pregame warmups, we eyed the confident Woodston players yucking it up and strutting; their first two games had been thirty-point blowouts. They were dribbling between their legs and throwing passes behind their backs. We shot our lay-ups and practice shots before retreating to the bench for our final huddle.

"Okay, you have seen them. Numbers 34 and 25 are their two best ball handlers. Make them pick up their dribble and try to not let them past mid-court. They are cocky and think we will be another blowout. We are going to hit them with the press on any completed free throw and any time they take the ball out. On a defensive rebound, quickly get to your spot to pester them at all times. Johnny, no one gets behind you. Got that? Jimmy and Layton, you dog them on every pass in, and use your quickness to steal the ball. Alan, you and Steve should be able to pick off the ball. Then pass to each other and we should be able to get layups at our end," Coach Clayton said as if believing this plan would come off without a hitch.

The teams took center court. The Woodston players were tall. It was hard to imagine that they only weighed 95 pounds. One guy made twenty points in their last game. Then there was their ball handler. He was fast. Another one was the passer. We had them all identified as the opening tip was thrown.

Sloppy passes, interceptions, traveling, double dribbles, and a confused deer-in-the-headlights look came to this over-confident, cocky opponent. The full court press had totally disrupted a once very formidable, unbeatable foe. How could a defense put in at literally the last minute cause such a Goliath to fall? The game was not even close. Woodston lost their composure and was never able to figure out the press. The smaller, better-coached team would stand for the team photo with the first-place trophy. The midgets had confused and conquered the giants.

Grandstanding always remained with me as a shamed method of drawing attention to myself. I had learned a lesson, though I was not aware of it until it was pointed out by a wonderful coach and principal, Charles Clayton. He taught us that winning and losing were not the most important things. We did our fair share of both, but, the most important value learned for my life was in how I played the game.

ഇൗ

James Kenyon

THE FARM CAT

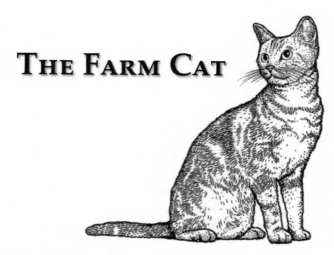

Our farm was different than most. We had more cats, prettier cats, nicer cats, and healthier cats that any farm around.

"But, Daddy," I screamed. "Why do they do it?"

"I'm so sorry son. I really can't answer that. I just remember that wild, stray tom cats always killed my kittens too when I was your age," he said.

"But why do they just kill them and leave their bodies?" I pled for a reason. With tears dribbling down on my tee shirt, I cried. "I hate tom cats, Daddy."

"I do too," he agreed. "But don't let your mother hear you say the word hate."

I picked up the four, soft, lifeless kittens to bury them out in the hackberry tree windbreak. Placing their bodies in a shoebox lined with a piece of Mother's felt sewing remnants, I closed the lid and covered the box with a piece of scrap tin so the other animals could not dig up the remains. I placed sand and pine needles over the grave. Mounding and packing the dirt, I placed a lathe marker on which I had printed with a crayon, the date and contents of the burial plot.

Springtime is the kitten time of year because mother cats come into heat in the late winter. The timing had to be related to the lengthening of the day. I was puzzled at hearing the screaming, yowling sounds at night in the distant barns and sheds. I never quite understood the cat courting scene, but had seen tom cats jump on my wonderful mother cats at feeding times. Quicker than I could turn around, they would hop on a female that was stopped and lying on her stomach. The tom would bite the female cat's neck and lay on her back. In less time than I could take off my cap and try to shoo them away, the deed was done. The tom sauntered off and looked back at me with evil eyes. He seemed to be saying, "I'll be back when you are not here. So just you see!"

I walked home from school—a short, ten-minute jaunt—on a cloudless April afternoon. I knew it was going to be one of the best days of my life. Yellow Mamma had such a big tummy the night before when she sat waiting for her milk from supper. I missed seeing her that morning as I had quickly milked the cows and finished the other chores. I cleaned up and headed out the door for school, knowing she must have had her kittens overnight.

Banging the porch door closed behind me, I called out, "Mommy, I'm home." I threw down my books and changed clothes. I headed out the door knowing there must have been kittens born overnight. With the screen door banging shut, I started my kitten hunt. It did not take long to hit pay dirt. In the cow barn, in front of the manger about three feet off the ground, a nest was perfectly molded in the side of the hay. Chickens had made the nest to lay their eggs. This time, the nest was filled by the gray tabby mother cat curled around four scrawny babies nursing away. I had seen that she was fat too, but this was a surprise. I thought I would find Old Yeller. I had learned before that if I ogled too much, or touched the kittens, the mother would grab them by the nape of the neck and hide them in another place the next day. This instinct was always fascinating to observe, but I just peeked, praised her, and headed out for the next treasure hunt.

It did not take long. Climbing up into the hayloft, Old Yeller came meandering down to greet me. She meowed and stretched, showing her gaunt abdomen. I petted her and she purred immediately. We talked and she cocked her head, seeming to say, "Do you want to see my kittens?" If cats could talk, she seemed to motion me with her head, and we scampered up to the top of the hay mow. There were her four newborns all curled up in a neat ball. With the evening sun casting shadows through the four-pane side window, the cobwebs glistened in the rays.

What a day! I had never had eight newborns in one day. Could it be that there were more? I got the bucket and methodically gathered the eggs. As the large brown eggs began to fill the bucket, I remembered to look for the stray nest high up in the hayshed. Scrambling over the hay bales, I could not believe my eyes. There was Black Momma. She looked up at me and meowed.

"Well, lookie here. How did you expect me to find you hidden in the hay stack?" I whispered softly. Maybe this was just a defense to hide the kittens from attack by the tom cats.

Black Momma seemed to smile as she closed her eyes. Four coal black kittens wiggled in position to wrestle for an open nipple. I patted her on the head and backed away quickly. No eggs were found, but the third nest of kittens was incredible.

I carried the eggs to the house. I exchanged the egg bucket for two galvanized milk buckets and headed back to the cow barn. I placed the measured grain in the manger for the three milk cows. I nonchalantly peeked in to see Grey Kitty's newborns. I flipped up the hook to let the cows in to be milked. Swissy, Black Baldy, and Red Bomber marched into their stanchions with their normal clamor.

Dad stopped in to see how the milking was going. I had the radio going and the cats who did not have new families were all sitting on their haunches, awaiting the occasional squirt of milk from me. I looked up to see Dad, not missing a stroke of milking. I beamed. "Dad, you wouldn't believe what I have found tonight. Not one. Not two. But three litters of kittens tonight. Can you believe it?"

Dad chuckled with a gleam in his eyes. "Well, have you been to the corn crib yet? If not, you may want to check the crib when you finish milking," he said, baiting me. I had an inkling of what he implied, but hardly believed it possible.

The milk cows were kicked out of the barn. The barn swallows had already started their mud daubed nests and chattered away over my head, sitting on the electric wires. The peach trees were in full bloom as I paused to take in all the wonder of spring on my perfect farm day.

I delivered the milk to the house and then set out for one more treasure hunt. There in the corner of the empty, slatted corncrib, curled up in a gunny sack, was Little Tabby. Unbelievably, there were one, two, three, and—yes—four sleeping kittens. This was an over-the-top evening to find four litters with four kittens each.

Babies of any species were cute and precious. Sixteen kittens clamoring for their share around a pan of milk was quite a sight. There would never be any vaccinations or worming for this herd. There were no ear mite treatments or veterinarians giving advice. The love and survival of the fittest for farm kitties was the most that was ever given.

This mass production and over-population did not go unnoticed by my mother. There were thirty-two mouths to feed by mid-summer. Mother gave me instructions on treating kittens with goober eyes—inflamed with a mucous discharge, eyes closed and sealed by a hard, scabby crust. The kittens would have the sniffles and blow bubbles from their nose. I learned to clean their eyes with diluted salt water and swabbed them with a cotton ball. It only took a few days and the reddened, pustular eyes started to look better. I learned years later as a veterinarian that we had been treating a virus called rhinotracheitis. Instead of watching kittens die, I saw them recover from this upper respiratory virus. It was remarkable as a veterinarian to have had this experience treating sick kittens. When my colleagues thought that there was no hope for the crusty-eyed kitten, I knew that they could recover with supportive care.

Overnight, there was a sudden reduction in the cat population. Half of the cats disappeared. My mother may have been the responsible one, though no one ever called her on the deed. Had she possibly had someone come and haul off my wonderful kittens? Had distemper struck, and the youngest cats been affected and died a miserable death? I never knew the answer. Though I loved every one of them the same, the sheer numbers of kittens were beyond manageable.

The day of sixteen newborns kittens nursing with their mothers was a hallmark in my young life. How many stray tom cats were in action at the same time? That was also a wonder. Those days of lying on my back on the padded, backyard grass, being swamped by dozens of purring cats was the ultimate fix.

ଛଠଢ

THIS LITTLE PIGGY

"Jimmy!" My dad shook me from a deep sleep. "Uncle Ivan has a fire. Quick, get your boots on. We must go to see what we can do." Dad beckoned in his hurried, but gentle, voice. My dad was never an alarmist, but when he said hurry, I knew it was serious. No questions were asked. I heeded and rushed out the back door to meet the pickup truck. The beams of the headlights bounced like a search light, penetrating the thick layers of smoke. The smell was acrid, unlike any forest fire or campfire smoke I had known. I jumped into the truck and tied my boots as we pulled away from the house.

As we sped through town, I heard the sirens blaring like an air raid was coming. In just a few minutes, we arrived in Uncle Ivan's driveway. The crunchy gravel beneath the tires was the only noise in the fire lit night. Ahead, the small, wooden-framed farrowing house was in full blaze. It was as if an accelerant had been poured over the entire surface and every portion of the building had been torched. There were no pigs running or screaming out of the inferno. There was no attempt to extinguish the flames. A garden hose sprinkle would not have made a difference. There were neighbors standing in a semicircle, watching silently as they all knew there was nothing to be done. The crackling and popping of the fire sent sparks high into the air like fireworks exploding. The burnt orange light reflected on the spectators' glasses; women huddled with blankets over their shoulders.

Dad and I spotted Uncle Ivan in the distance trying to unravel a kinked garden hose. "Here, let me help you, Ivan," my dad calmly offered.

"I know it is useless for the hog house, but we've got to get some water on the cow barn in case one of those embers lands on its roof," Ivan directed.

Farm building fires were usually total losses as the dry, wooden structures were like powder kegs. Farrowing house fires were common. Heat lamps hung over a nursing sow to provide warmth in the make-shift farrowing pens had ignited the fire. With dusty straw bedding, care had to be taken with heat lamps to avoid direct contact with the straw. A rambunctious sow might throw her head causing a dangling heat lamp to light a piece of straw. The inferno became inevitable.

All that was left from the fire were smoldering embers. In the quietness of the night air, a squealing noise was tracked to a rusted-out barrel in the line of shrubs against a distant fence. I heard the noise first, and motioned Dad's attention to the mournful, faint squealing sound. With a flashlight, we located a pitiful little pig, nearly lifeless, shivering in the protection of the barrel.

"Oh, Dad. Look at him. He's scalded and burned all over. I'm going to run to the truck to get a gunny sack to keep him warm," I blurted as I darted off.

I returned to find dad holding the small piglet. We wrapped him up and I carried him in my arms back to the warmth of the front seat of the pickup. Dad scouted the surrounding farmstead for any other stragglers that may have survived the fire. There were none to be found. All told, six sows and some fifty nursing piglets had perished. Only one little five-pound squealer was left to remind us of the blazing death trap.

We drove back home with this little pig I called Porky. I found an old towel in the rag bag to give him a more comfortable cover. A peach crate on the back porch was emptied, and Dad and I made a bed for this stunned little creature. Mother gave us some Vaseline to rub over his now hairless, singed, and burned crimson body.

"Do you give him a chance, Dad?" I softly asked.

"Well, he's made it this far. We'll just have to put the Vaseline on him and see," he said with caution.

Porky's whimpering and shivering was a sad reminder of his ordeal. I filled an empty plastic bottle with hot water and placed it in the peach crate to provide Porky some warmth throughout the night.

At the first light of dawn, I crawled out of bed. My feet were chilled on the shiny waxed linoleum floor as I hurried to check on Porky. I removed the top towel cover over the box and smiled, "Ya' little Porky. Look at you this morning. You are all snuggled here with your hot water bottle. I bet you're hungry, aren't you?"

Dad heard me talking and cracked the door open to the porch to see that Porky had indeed made roll call. "Son, it looks like we need to get this little guy some breakfast," he said.

Man, did Porky love cow's milk. The warmer, the better. I first fed him with a baby bottle. He would lay back in my arms and even try to help hold the bottle with his front feet. The foam in the corners of his mouth glistened as he smacked the nipple with gusto.

I applied the Vaseline salve to his burned skin to keep it moist and covered for several days. The scabby surface layer became hard and crusty. It started to peel and fall-off in chunks. A new layer of shiny pink skin was uncovered, and little bristles of hair emerged with minimal scarring.

Porky soon outgrew his peach crate on our back porch. His plaintive squealing soon drew the ire of Mother. I made a small pen in our farrowing house for Porky. He learned to drink his milk from a pan, though his bottle nursing had left him imprinted on me. Two months after the fire, Porky returned to my Uncle Ivan's farm. Parting with my friend was difficult. I shed no tears, but I had to bite the inside of my cheek as he was placed in the big cardboard box in the pickup bed. I was in total agreement that he had to go back home. I fully knew what happened when pigs grew up. This little piggy would have to go to market, and I would not have liked that scene.

This little piggy had been special on our farm. He had a name and was bottle fed. Generally, pigs multiplied rapidly on a farm. Each sow could have twenty pigs each year. Naming each of them was not a reasonable undertaking. There could be favorite sows, but by the time the little pigs were placed into the fattening lot, they all looked and acted the same. A hog wallow or mud-hole was a favorite cooling place for pigs. Whether the water came from a flooded, over-run stock tank or a convenient garden hose, there was no relief like a soothing mud bath from a scorching Kansas sun. With only a snout and ear above the surface, these porkers could be mistaken for submerged hippopotamuses in the Serengeti.

Pigs and shoats (young pigs) were offered cracked cornmeal mix in a gravity-drop, self-feeder. Pigs ate any time, day or night. The individual, metal trough lids banged as the pigs left each feeding station compartment. Pigs were much like human infants; when they weren't sleeping, they were eating.

Morning, noon, and night, I carried buckets of water and poured them into a long, hand-made wooden trough. Garbage and left-overs from the school lunch program or whey from the local cheese plant were like dessert for the ravenous, growing pigs. These liquids were called slop. Slopping the pigs at noon in the stifling summer days was a crucial requirement.

After seeing how much the pigs liked the sour smelling whey, I had a plan. I found a fifty-five gallon, empty oil drum barrel. I filled it half full of cracked corn and topped it with water. Several times a day, I stirred the concoction with a shovel handle, making sure to mix the sediment well. In no time at all, the sour slurry started to smell and looked like something the pigs would like for a treat. Dipping into the barrel with a bucket, I carefully ladled out the corn mash and poured it into the long water troughs. Slurping the mash like chocolate addicts, the pigs lined up three-deep for their noontime thirst quench. Moonshine and stills were against the law at the time, but divvying out a few pints to each pig did not seem to harm anyone. With only a few slurps, comically staggering, oinking, grunting pigs plopped themselves in the shade for an afternoon siesta.

The key to this festive party was to keep adding more corn and water to the barrel and stirring the home brew several times each day. It was like making sour dough pancake mix. As long as the yeast was given more starch and sugar, the intoxicating beverage kept flowing. My dad didn't seem to mind my experimenting with this home brew slop. Neither of us told Mother as I am sure she would have tsk-tsked us and threatened to call the Women's Christian Temperance Union.

Porky had been nursed back to life. He was the only pig on our farm to ever have a name. He had sucked from a bottle with such character. He had learned to squeal in such a begging manner to get his way. The cow's milk helped to save his life. I am sure he would have grunted and become addicted to some of my home brew. Happy hour with this farmer boy's porridge would have made Porky smile.

One late afternoon, I found a possum starting to suck chicken eggs in the cow barn manger. I grabbed a pointed broom handle and poked at him. His ugly eyes penetrated the shadows. He hissed and the hair raised up along his back. True to form for a possum, he went limp and rolled out of the nest like he was dead. But, I was up to his tricks. I watched his steady deep breaths give away his faked death. I scooped up this seemingly lifeless varmint in a shovel and took him out to the driveway. I was determined to end his egg-sucking days, even if that meant ending his life. Motionless, he laid there in the shovel. With all my strength, I pitched Mr. Possum as high into the air as I could and watched as he came crashing to the ground. After several flops on the roadway, it became obvious that this prehistoric looking creature had some life-preserving features. He was no bigger than a large cat. Did he also have nine lives? At the apex of each free ride into the air, he effortlessly repositioned his legs. When he hit the ground, his legs softened the concussion. He never once showed any life or any other movement. Was he dead, or was he just playing possum?

I needed a final test for this little predator to confirm that his earthly life had ended. I considered tossing him into the cow stock water tank. That would have required fishing his body out if he truly was deceased. There had to be another method. Ah, what about throwing him into the hog pen to see if the pigs could rouse him?

Approaching the pigs who were squealing in anticipation for the noon-day hooch, my shovel full of possum brought them all to attention. I flipped the lifeless, furry, rat-tailed varmint into the mass of waiting porkers. It was like watching Lazarus rise from the grave. Mr. Possum sprang to life in a hissing, acrobatic move, and landed on the back of a startled pig. He wobbled and leapt onto another back like a logger on a log roll. He finally split the scene and scurried under the fence, never to be seen again. I never imagined a possum could move so fast.

ಸಂ

FARMER BOY'S FIRST KISS

"Who is your girlfriend?"

"Come on, tell me who your girlfriend is."

Was it the culture of the Baby Boomer parents or grandparents? Was it the teenage weddings in the post-war era? This was a frequent question heard from uncles or family acquaintances. Not that these were pressuring inquiries, but most school-age children could answer, at least, that they had a special friend who was of the opposite gender.

As for this farmer boy, I had limited choices. The prettiest girl near my age was a second cousin. Scratch that one from consideration. The next in line happened to be one of just three girls in the first-grade class. She was blonde, petite, sweet, nice, smiled, and dressed well. Gracie's blond hair was so fine and coiffed that it seemed silvery and wavy. In her pretty, button-down, green-checkered dresses, she was angelic. She was awarded the back-row desk due to her good behavior. Mrs. Adams still had her thumb on me, so I was never able to sit next to Gracie and ogle at her porcelain white complexion.

Gracie was nearly perfect, but there was one problem. Three other boys in the first grade also thought she was beautiful. Five days of seeing her in school and another day at Sunday school made it almost a perfect week. All four boys in our class vied for her attention. It became quite the conversation as others asked the question, "So, is Gracie your girlfriend?"

It never came to blows, but out and out wrestling matches were fought over Gracie. David moved away in the second grade and the competition was reduced to only three. Throughout this quest, Gracie seemed oblivious to our attraction and was smiling and sweet to all. It never came to physical contact, no holding hands or playground smooching, but playing alone at recess with Gracie was special.

We showed off for her attention by riding our bicycles while standing on the seat. Putting cards in the bicycle spokes as noise makers seemed to make no impression. Athletic prowess in basketball or soccer did not seem to impress Gracie, either. Being a good speller or good singer did not attract her praise.

Then the unthinkable happened. Gracie moved away. I'm sure I was not the only boy who wrote her a letter addressed to her new town of Oberlin. And I was not the only one who signed my name beneath the word love. No letter was ever returned, addressee unknown, and no note from Gracie was ever received by any of the three boys who loved her.

The rather annoying inquiries persisted.

School dances did not really encourage boy-girl interaction. The boys all sat around the perimeter of the lunch room/dance floor. The girls danced together until they were brave enough to ask a boy to dance. Such a request was not turned down. An awkward refusal seemed more embarrassing than just getting up and trying to dance to the music.

In the late 1950s, rock and roll music was hitting the nation with wanton abandon. Elvis, the Everly Brothers, Buddy Holley, and Chubby Checker records were collected and played in everyone's basements. Birthday parties with crepe paper streamers, spinning globe lights, and darkened rooms reduced the inhibition of timid boys.

Hay rides were sponsored by 4-H Clubs, church youth groups, and school functions. A slow-moving Farmall tractor with its lights bouncing in the dusk pulled a hayrack lined with straw bales and several dozen kids from the parking lot. As the crimson sun dropped beneath the crested, western horizon, the tractor puttered and pulled the party-on-wheels to a distant grove of trees or a sandbar on the river for a hotdog and marsh-mallow roast. Hands would be held. Blankets would be wrapped around shoulders. Pairing off boys and girls soon became obvious. Darkness had a way of stimulating the attraction between these couples.

Girls from another town were always more intriguing than the ones we already knew well from school. Asking some girl to accompany me to a church youth event or hayride was special, especially if she was from out of town. Countywide church hayrides widened the playing field extensively. I met sweet Jeri-lyn on such an occasion. I was twelve, and she just happened to be a year older. She was adorable. She had dimples when she smiled with the cutest, inviting welcome. Her powder-puff blue eyes danced with excitement. She was a few inches shorter than me, could run fast, and was not shy in the least. We held hands under the red and black checkered blanket next to a flickering campfire. We talked as if we had known each other forever. She was so comfortable to be with and sweet. I was beginning to think this religion and church stuff was all right!

Since Jerilyn lived in the town of the county seat, seeing her often posed a problem. I would call her and we would talk for an hour at a time on the phone. It was not considered polite or proper for a girl to call a boy in those days. Jerilyn invited me to the Midway Theater for a Saturday afternoon movie. My parents arranged to get me to Hill City in time to meet her. She waited coyly in the lobby of the movie theater for me.

Somewhere after the newsreel and the Bugs Bunny cartoon, she looped her arm around mine on the arm rest. Wow, this touch was exhilarating, but I never took my eyes off the movie screen. She laid her head on my shoulder. My heart did a flip.

Seeing me as an adolescent, slowly maneuvering in an attempt to put my arm around Jerilyn in the adjoining seat surely must have been comical. By the time my arm made it around her neck and shoulder, it was extended backward. The movie goer sitting behind us two lovebirds would have found their line of sight obscured.

How could things get better that this? It didn't take long. This beautiful, innocent, dimple-faced girl reached across my chest and kissed me like I had never been kissed before. It was not a peck. It was not a smooch. It was a kiss like she knew what she was doing. I was in love and the movie was over way too soon. As we left the darkened theater and reemerged into the bright, late afternoon sunlight, we squinted to see that our rides were waiting to pick us up.

More phone calls ensued. Letters crossed in the mail. Several more smooch-filled movies kept us in touch, so to speak. The ten-mile separation may as well have been one-hundred. Farm work, baseball, and a summer away from activities were all deterrents to regular meetings. A few more movies and a hayride in the fall kept the romance active. The county 4-H fair and rodeo allowed for three straight days of seeing each other. Since the fair was in Hill City, Jerilyn attended every day. Her sandy-blonde hair was pulled into a pony tail. She donned a light blue cap to shade her from the August sun. She wore white, sleeveless, button-down shirts and white tennis shoes without socks. In my cowboy hat, tight-fitting Wrangler jeans, and cowboy boots, I was always in motion. The livestock I entered at the fair were in three different buildings and required constant attention. Feeding the pigs, chickens, and three show steers twice daily with a girlfriend in tow was special. Taking these animals in the show ring with a girl leaning on the pipe fence railing, beaming her approval, made this farmer boy excel in showmanship. We held hands as I accompanied her to the carnival. We rode the tall Ferris wheel. She screamed as we rode the roller coaster with my arm around her, securely protecting her from danger.

The shooting galleries became my most frequently visited booth at the arcade. The carney man would start the rotating, floating duck parade on the distant wall. One by one, with bulls-eye aim, I picked off the yellow metal ducks in sequence. My days shooting sparrows and rifle target shooting really paid in dividends. I knew which BB guns had proper sights and won many teddy bear prizes for my admiring friend. After winning the fourth teddy bear, the carney man gave me an offer that I knew I couldn't refuse.

"If you buy one more round of shooting and win again, I'll give you that big white bear and you turn the other four bears back in. If you don't win, you have to give me back the other four bears anyway," he said, clever in his challenge. I grinned at my Jerilyn. Sweat beads glistened on the bridge of her nose. She seemed enthralled at the attention and thought that her duck shooter could win the biggest teddy bear she had ever seen.

"Okay, you're on," I said, confident in the acceptance of his challenge. I selected my gun carefully, loaded the ventral BB cylindrical barrel, and shouted, "start 'em up!" Aim, blink, cock the handle, aim, and blink again. Cock the handle, aim, blink... over and over. All ten ducks were down. The coveted white bear with the red bow was Jerilyn's and I was her hero.

The phone calls continued. Pictures on my desk and in my billfold reminded me of how pretty she was. I was not embarrassed to answer the age-old question. Indeed, I did have a girlfriend.

Loving and losing seemed to have its way. The next summer, Jerilyn sadly reported to me that she was moving away with her family to Prescott, Kansas. We exchanged several love letters, but their frequency became less with time. One perfumed Hallmark card came at Christmas. Jerilyn said she had a new boyfriend, but if she was not married by the time she got out of high school some three years later, maybe we could get back together. No tears were shed, but the image of the dimples and her pretty face would never go away. Our paths were to never cross again. Jerilyn was gone, but remembering her still makes me smile.

> As time goes by
> You must remember this
> A kiss is just a kiss
> A sigh is just a sigh
> The fundamental things apply
> As time goes by
>
> *lyrics by Herman Hupfield,*
> *song by Frank Sinatra*

ಬಂಃ

James Kenyon

FARMER BOY THE PRESIDENT

Bang! Down came the gavel on the cardboard table. I called the meeting to order. "Please rise and face the flag and say the Pledge of Allegiance with me," I announced, twelve years old and the new 4-H club president. All fifteen members of the Bogue Blazers and their leaders solemnly rose with right hands over hearts, reciting the Pledge. As president of the club, I was no longer able to be disruptive, whispering in the back row. It took my full attention to follow the agenda.

"Now would you join me in the 4-H Pledge?" Starting with their heads, the club members progressed through heart, hands, and health.

4-H was established during the early 1900s. Clubs spread across the nation and provided youth from eight to eighteen years old the opportunity to learn, inform, and experience leadership. The club meetings were very formal and followed *Robert's Rules of Order* for parliamentary procedure. The format prepared 4-H members for organizational meetings from corporate to school board meetings, business they would experience and attend to for the rest of their lives. The call to order, the secretary's minutes, treasurer's report, project reports, demonstrations, old business, new business, and unfinished business were presented in pretty much the same order for every club across America.

The program for 4-H club meetings was by the individual young members. A talk or demonstration by one or more of the members, selected from his or her projects for the year, helped all in attendance to learn. These projects ranged from cooking, sewing, gardening, livestock, photography, and carpentry. The demonstration reports were on any topic that the member chose. This allowed the member to stand up in front of the club, describe the demonstration, and perform it.

Knees would shake as each month's program featured a different 4-H report. Memorization was encouraged and reading the report was discouraged. Posters with headings, pictures, and diagrams made these programs more interesting. For five minutes, it gave the 4-H member the opportunity to tell of his or her project and enabled practice standing on their own and instructing others.

Members were taught to stand firm on two feet and eliminate the 'ums' and 'and-uhs' from their speech. Eye contact and leadership were learned, even for the shyest, youngest members.

The 4-H year was highlighted by several main events. County 4-H Days, Regional 4-H Days, and the summer 4-H County Fair were among the highlights. Interaction with other clubs and learning the names of up to two-hundred other 4-H members was all a part of the large network of learning and leadership opportunities. Ornery boys, mischievous acts, cliques, and immature behavior were frowned upon.

Attending the 4-H camp was every member's rite of passage. A short week at Rocks Springs Ranch near Junction City, Kansas, some two-hundred miles away from home, was exciting. At camp we experienced and participated in organized activities like swimming, sporting groups, horseback riding, rifle range, and crafts. Eating in a large mess hall, we met and interacted with 4-H members from perhaps twenty other counties from all over the state. Sleeping accommodations were in segregated, raised, fixed tents. More than one frog would somehow sneak into some squeamish girl's bed roll.

Some of the braver campers snuck out at night. Not that there was anything to do; but with a flashlight and some imagination, prowling around camp made us feel free and daring. Never being caught in the act was the most important part of the prank. More than one raid on the camp freezer provided ice cream bars to the marauding camp juveniles. Brave girls were coaxed out from their tents and made these escapades seem even more adventurous.

My 4-H projects started with a baby beef, gardening, and chickens. Each project had to include the planning, project book, details of costs, tracking of expenses and profit, and a summary of the benefit to the family. The project book was a year-end summary of what the 4-H member had learned.

The baby beef project began each November following the roundup and weaning of the spring calves. The calf with the most frame and best confirmation was selected. These steer calves were about five hundred pounds at this time. After separating the calf from the weanling pen of calves, it was moved to a small pen in the cow barn. Dad would throw a lariat rope loop around its neck and we pulled the calf next to a post. They would fight this restraint and throw their bodies at us, trying to get free.

"It's alright, calfie." Dad tried to assure this frightened dynamo. "No, no, no, take it easy. Slow. Slow," he said, softly talking to the young steer. "Okay, now don't choke yourself down. Jimmy, give me a little slack or he's going to choke."

"Are you ready for the halter?" I awaited directions.

"I think so. We've about worn him out," Dad would say.

Placing the rope halter on the head with a chin-chain for tightening the lead rope was the first act in teaching the calf how to lead. Tied to a sturdy support post, the animal was allowed to pull back hard until his eyes bulged. As the calf started to feel pressure over his muzzle, it would snort and blow his nose on me, then it would relax and quickly lunge forward to get instant relief, only to pull back hard again with all four feet planted and digging in to see if it could pull the post over. I would stand beside him and curry him with a brush comb. I sometimes had to dodge a quick jab from a rear, side-kicking foot. I placed a firm hand on the quivering body to let the calf know I was not going to hurt it. I talked the whole time, trying to calm and soothe him.

"Hey, you little dickens. I'm not going to hurt you. Easy. Easy. Now that's better," I said to encourage the free-spirited dogie. The smooth, rounded, rope halter was left on him for the next eight months. Tying the calf up every couple of weeks assured some training and respect for pressure on a lead rope.

The best time to pet and curry a calf was when they were eating. The ground corn ration was placed in the chest-high feed bunk with a liquid molasses topping. A calf licking molasses is like a kid with an ice cream cone. The grain is licked up and the bottom of the wooden feed bunk is left shiny from the continued cleaning with the tongue.

A calf has a spot on both sides of the tail head in the coccygeal fossa that is a sweet spot for sensation. Rubbing this area gently will cause them to curl their tail to the opposite side. Softly massaging one side and then the other will cause the calf to turn its whole rear end for the scintillating massage. This was a true sign that there is progress in the taming and developing of a show calf's trust and friendship with the farmer boy.

Snapping the lead rope into the chin-chain, I carefully led the calf in tight circles in his pen. An occasional, wild-running spin would take us around the pen in a panicked frenzy. More reassurance and petting calmed the calf for the repetitive circles.

Petting, molasses, currying, and soft talking to my calf occurred each night as part of my chores. Keeping the calf inside and out of the sunlight was a way of growing the hair longer. Longer hair for the show calf could be brushed and coiffed to make the legs and sides more prominent and attractive in the show ring. I never quite mastered this long-hair growing technique for my calves.

By the time school was out in the spring, I walked the calf daily to fully train him to lead. If the calf balked, bucked, or charged wildly, I wrapped the lead rope around a tree to regain control of the steer.

4-H calves received weekly baths with the garden hose, spraying down the steer while it was tied to an elm tree. Soaping and scrubbing with a brush seemed to make them feel like a bath was a treat. Being careful not to frighten with the water shooting from the hose, I could wash and clean a calf in no time at all. Before long, they drank cold water from the hose just like a human slurping the cool liquid refreshment.

The best part of the baby beef project came the first week of August with the Graham County 4-H Fair and Rodeo. The livestock was brought to the fairgrounds on a Sunday night and the fair took place the next three days. My chickens, pigs, and baby beef were unloaded at the fairgrounds. The steer was tied to a ring in the fence where he stood in belly-deep straw. The new smells and activity made this now 1,000-pound buddy fidgety and wild eyed. I slept in a bedroll next to my calf to give the steer assurance.

Eying the other entries, I would size up the competition. My pride was that all my calves were selected from our cow herd and not purchased at a club calf auction. These calves were truly a product of my dad's breeding selections rather than from a large, commercial calf-selling operation. Blue, red, and white ribbons were earned. I got my share of red and white placings, but the blue ribbons came in later years as the style of preferred baby beef changed to longer and taller show calves.

In the early 1950s, the Hereford breed was selected for short, squatty frames. My dad never went that way in his bull selection. He did buy one bull that threw smaller, short calves. One calf was born as a dwarf and never got bigger that three-hundred pounds as a mature steer. This was a terrible recessive gene to have in our herd. This bull was soon sold. A dwarf and the effects of breeding specific characteristics made me a young believer in genetic selection.

I loved each calf differently for the next nine years of taking baby beef projects. I never named any of them. The time of training, feeding, leading, and bathing was quite a bonding experience, but on the last day of the fair, the steer would be led into the auction ring to be purchased by a local business sponsor.

"This is Jimmy Kenyon leading his blue-ribbon calf that weighs 1,140 pounds. Who'll give me 500, now 550, and a 6, now 650?" The auctioneer chanted into his microphone. Over the loud speaker, his nasal tone continued with the rattling cadence until there were no other bidders. "And it is sold to bidder number twenty-one, and that would be Farmers State Bank of Bogue, and a big thank you to Mr. Kirkpatrick."

I led my steer out of the ring, removed the show halter, and patted him on the rear as he ran down the runway. I never cried, but I usually did have a lump in my throat. Dad would put his hand on my shoulder. He knew not to try to make me talk.

"Nice job son. We may not have won the purple ribbon, but he was representative of our herd and we can be proud of that," Dad would say with encouragement.

"Yep. Just think, he was so wild that first day we threw the lariat on him. I think he was beautiful. I'll never forget his yellowish hair coat. Man, did he love the molasses!" I would say, biting my lip as we walked away from the sale barn. "I love you, Dad. Thanks for helping me select him. I think this year's calves are going to be even better."

"How about us stopping at Buck's grill for a pop?" Dad smiled as he knew I always had a craving for a Nesbitt orange pop.

I pledge my head to clearer thinking,
My heart to greater loyalty,
My hands to larger service,
My health to better living,
For my club, my community, my country, and my world.
The 4-H Pledge

മോരു

FARMER BOY

THE POLITICIAN

My mother was the county Republican chairwoman. Thus, we had governors, representatives, and aspiring office holders in our home frequently.

The 1960 presidential election between Kennedy and Nixon was a watershed of many proportions. The ugliest was that the difference of religion surfaced as an issue in politics. One intriguing vacancy was for the Kansas First District United States Congressional seat. Wint Smith from Smith Center was not running for reelection. There had been a redistricting and Kansas was losing a congressional seat. An incumbent, Democrat Lowell Breeding from Southwest Kansas Second District, was running in the newly drawn First District.

Two prominent Republican county attorneys were seeking their party's nomination. Bob Dole from Russell and Keith Sebelius from Norton were both in our home vying for Mother's support. Bob Dole was charming and the most persistent. He went on to win the primary election against Sebelius and the general election against Representative Breeding. Dole's place in American politics began in western Kansas. He went on to lead the national Senate as both the minority and majority leader for many years. Most would compare Dole to Henry Clay or some of the country's greatest senators. He had access and extremely good relations with both parties. He was a great compromiser, respected and loved by both his Republican and Democratic colleagues.

Bob Dole ran for president two times. He gave campaign stump speeches all over the country. I met him twice in Iowa, my oldest sister met him twice in Texas, another sister met him once in Wisconsin, and my older brother met him once in Kansas City. Upon hearing my last name, he would say, "You must be Anita Kenyon's son from Bogue. I meet you Kenyon's all over the country!" What recall he had to pull up my mother's name from thirty-five years before.

When I made an ill-fated attempt for the Iowa House of Representatives in 2012, I contacted Dole's office in Washington to get an endorsement letter. Senator Chuck Grassley was the honored speaker at my fundraising event. When he saw the letter that Bob Dole sent me, Chuck was amazed and incredulous. Grassley and I have remained friends, and I admire his efforts and contributions to our country, much like Dole's.

Not one of my experiences as a boy growing up on a farm, but the culmination of having a dad and mother who taught by example, and allowed freedom for expression, exploration, and leadership, led me to where I am today. I did not make it to the State House, but many other callings have filled my commitment to community service. Being a grandparent of four (soon to be five) has been one of my life's greatest joys. My three dear, successful children are the pride of my life. My wife of nearly one half century has been a mutual loving partner. We are shooting for another three decades. The lessons of integrity, honesty, commitment and responsibility to care for others and for animals—honed in my childhood growing up on a farm— led me to my chosen profession as veterinarian, a career I have found both satisfying and rewarding in many ways.

ℝ℞

BOB DOLE
THE ATLANTIC BUILDING
950 F STREET, N.W., 10TH FLOOR
WASHINGTON, D.C. 20004

September 3, 2012

Dear Jim,

First, I want to wish you luck and secondly thank Chuck Grassley for hosting this event.

We met a long time ago in Bogue, Kansas. Your mother was my chairman in Graham County and you were almost a teenager.

I know the good people of Iowa pretty well and a majority helped me in the Presidential Primary in 1988 and 1996. Now your friends and your hard work will make you a winner in just a few weeks.

Public service can be rewarding and you will have an opportunity, as a legislator, to make a difference in the lives of many Iowans. Your neighbor Senator Grassley is an example of an outstanding public servant.

I cannot be there but I wish you the best.

God Bless America,

BOB DOLE

P.S. Say 'hello' to Leon and Agnes for me.

James R. Kenyon, DVM
PC Box 1204
Cedar Falls, IA 50613

REFLECTIONS

The meadowlark's call and the cottonwood trees
a farm boy's values grew among these.
Lessons from animals all great and small
honesty, integrity to care for them all.

An uncle, a cousin, a coach, and a preacher
a horse, a dog, and many a teacher.
For from small saplings grow great oaks
purpose and direction given by his folks.

This towhead has grown,
but the seeds were all sown
like every sunrise, the days to be told
reflections in the pool, the ripples unfold.

James Kenyon

James Kenyon

ACKNOWLEDGMENTS

I would like to thank Dr. Judith Harrington, my "little city girl" for first encouraging me and then editing these farm boy stories.

I thank the readers and friends who so willingly took their time to proofread each story. They are Carolyn Stafford, Cynthia Kenyon, Judy Burfeind, Linda Haack, Kathy Barnes, Mary Lyman, and Kelsey Suys.

The painting for the cover is an original by my dear sister-in-law, Barbara Steward Kenyon. It depicts the scene and our "Home on the Range."

The graphic designs were by John Kenyon. His talents are immense and he diligently formed the images for each chapter.

James Kenyon

ABOUT THE AUTHOR

James Kenyon was born and raised on a third generation family grain and livestock farm. At the age of four, propped up on his knees to see over the steering wheel, he guided the family pickup truck as his father forked out feed for cattle. He drove the tractor solo by the age of seven in the hay field. James grew up caring for cattle, pigs, chickens, and horses near the small town of Bogue, Kansas, population 300. The birds, cats, dogs, frogs, and possums were all part of his experiences with nature.

Today, James is a veterinarian in a 35-year, mixed animal practice in a beautiful Iowa college town. He is a veterinarian for the Alaska Iditarod Dog Sled Race and a 24-year member of the school board, as well as its current president. He leads numerous community organizations including Rotary, church, library, museums, and historical society. He chaired the Iowa Veterinary Medical Association and State Veterinary Board of Examiners. He was named Iowa Veterinarian of the Year.

James is married to his college sweetheart from Kansas City. They have blended the farm and city in their life together. They have three children, four grandchildren, and numerous pets.

www.jamesrkenyon.com

James is also the author of *The Art of Listening to the Heart* (Ooly Booly Press, Chicago, IL, April 2017), a collection of true stories from his work as a veterinarian. The book is available from the author, in bookstores, and at online book retailers.

WWW.MEADOWLARK-BOOKS.COM

Meadowlark Books is an independent publisher, born of a desire to produce high-quality books for print and electronic delivery. Our goal is to create a network of support for today's independent author. We provide professional book design services, ensuring that the stories we love and believe in are presented in a manner that enhances rather than detracts from an author's work.

We look forward to developing a collection of books that focus on a Midwest regional appeal, via author and/or topic. We are open to working with authors of fiction, non-fiction, poetry, and mixed media. For more information, please visit us at www.meadowlark-books.com.

Also by Meadowlark Books

Made in the USA
Lexington, KY
12 September 2017